Putting Your
Money
To Work

Lana J. Chandler

Betterway Publications, Inc.
White Hall, Virginia

Published by Betterway Publications, Inc.
White Hall, VA 22987

Cover design by Deborah B. Chappell
Typography by East Coast Typography

Library of Congress Cataloging-in-Publication Data

Chandler, Lana J.
    Putting your money to work.

    Bibliography: p.
    Includes index.
    1. Banks and banking — United States.   2. Investments — United States.   I. Title.
HG2491.C45   1986   332.1'7'0973   86-18783
ISBN 0-932620-63-9 (pbk.)

Printed in the United States of America
0987654321

To Athalea Honaker,
good friend and relative,
for the affection you have always shown me.

ACKNOWLEDGMENT

*A special thanks to Jack Young and Steve Marcum,
two of the nicest bankers around,
for taking the time to help me.*

Contents

Introduction

D oing business at your friendly neighborhood bank isn't so simple anymore. A few years ago, the average person had a checking account and a savings account. The former paid 0% interest while the latter typically earned 5% interest compounded quarterly. Unless stocks and bonds were purchased through a brokerage house, investment options available to the average person were limited. You could open a savings account, buy U.S. Savings Bonds, or purchase CDs. Of course, in those days CDs earned little more than savings accounts, and there was no such thing as "variable rates."

What if you had several thousand dollars to invest but no taste for risk?

Government-issued securities (i.e., T-Bills, Treasury Notes, Treasury Bonds) were almost the only options available. Even today these investment options are still popular with many. For a small fee, such instruments can be purchased through most banks or brokerage houses. Along with tax advantages, Government securities usually afford slightly higher interest rates. Money invested in such assets, however, cannot be accessed by simply writing checks. Also, early liquidation can actually cost the investor since market conditions determine selling prices.

In short, banking used to be a pretty cut-and-dry business.

If we had to give you an abbreviated description of banking prior to the late 1970s, it'd be:

1. Interest rates were fairly constant.
2. Services, penalties and interest rates were tightly regulated by the federal government.
3. One bank pretty well resembled another.

Today, banks offer the average person quite an assortment of flexible and varied investment options. No longer do you need thousands of dollars to look into high yields and flexible investment plans. Checking accounts are an excellent example of modern-day diversity. Along with regular checking accounts which pay 0% interest, your local bank might very well offer a dozen or more different plans which afford check-writing capability. Interest rates, service charges, and ATM access can vary depending on average balances, number of checks allowed per month, overdraft protections, etc.

Sound complicated?

It can be if you're not aware of what's been happening in the banking industry during the past few years.

So *how* did banking become so complicated?

Deregulation.

We've all heard the term "deregulation," but what does it really mean to the average person?

For one thing, not all banks are alike anymore. To use a bit of poetic license, deregulation is enabling each bank to develop its own "personality." Although services are basically the same (i.e., checking, savings, CDs), the way they offer them varies. Competition is no longer based on who offers the prettiest match boxes or sends out the nicest calendars! It's money . . . what a bank pays or charges its customers. In other words, where and how you bank may mean substantial profits or losses to *you.*

"For the amount I've got, it's not worth the trouble to shop around."

EFFECTIVE ANNUAL YIELD FROM A CD PAYING 8%

Compounded:

Annually	8.000
Semiannually	8.160
Quarterly	8.243
Monthly	8.300
Weekly	8.322
Daily	8.328

$5,000 INVESTED AT 8%

Compounded:	Will Earn:
Annually	$400.00
Semiannually	408.00
Quarterly	412.15
Monthly	415.00
Weekly	416.10
Daily	416.40

Don't kid yourself! You don't have to be a millionaire to realize profits or losses from investment decisions. In fact, the poorer you are, the more every cent counts!

As you can see from our above example, just a difference in *when* money is compounded can result in an annual earnings difference of $16.40 on $5,000 invested at 8%. Although $16.40 isn't a fortune, it certainly helps out on the groceries! Leave the $5,000 and its interest earnings on deposit for 10 years and the difference between daily and annual compounding reaps $332.37.

It's hard to avoid banks. Keeping the "family fortune" tucked under a mattress isn't too wise nor is digging a hole in the back yard. The best solution is to learn your way through the banking maze. It's really not complicated. All it takes is a little education about a lot of big changes which have been going on.

We'll show you the difference between daily compounding and daily interest. Are savings accounts obsolete? Maybe they no longer effectively meet your needs. Why people choose to have more than one checking account is explained in easy-to-understand terms.

Tax advantages are possible. Invest in an IRA and reduce the Federal income tax bite. Interest earned on Government securities may also be tax free.

Keep pace with the interest market by investing in variable-rate CDs. Lock into long-term high yields when interest rates are up by purchasing fixed-rate instruments.

Trust departments aren't just for the rich. They can assist in the preparation of wills, settle estates, and manage rental property. If you run a small business, explore what they have to offer in the way of pension plans.

Want to try your luck in the stock market game? If you know which stocks you want to buy and you're not seeking a broker's advice, explore discount brokerage.

Anyone who receives a Social Security check has probably seen or heard the term "direct deposit." In other words, such funds can be automatically deposited into a specified account rather than mailed to your home in the form of a check. Social Security checks, however, aren't the only candidates for this increasingly popular service. Life insurance premiums are one interesting example. Premiums can often be paid via a direct deposit transaction.

Do you worry about making the car payment, house payment, Christmas Club deposit, etc. while on vacation? Consider authorizing your bank to automatically transfer funds when requested. As an extra bonus for subscribing to this service, some banks will reduce loan payments or increase rates on deposit accounts.

Safe deposit boxes are an economical way to secure valuables. Not only can you safely store important financial papers, but other assets can also be protected such as jewelry, rare coins, etc. Basically, when you rent a safe deposit box all you're doing is renting space in a bank's vault.

Safekeeping services are another way to secure some highly negotiable instruments. For example, if your bank offers discount brokerage services they may also provide safekeeping services. Rather than issuing you the actual stock certificates, perhaps a bank will offer to "safekeep" them in their own vault. Whether or not your bank charges extra for this service could be something worth exploring.

Who really owns an account? Ownership depends on how names are placed when an account is opened. Like any other asset, bank accounts too are owned. We'll show you how signature cards play a vital role when it comes time to make withdrawals.

Too many people think daily interest and daily compounding are the same. They aren't. How a bank compounds interest and the time-table it uses to calculate such interest are two *very* different topics. We'll show you how to understand what those slick marketing ads are really saying in terms of dollars and cents.

Several people may want to combine their funds to earn higher interest rates, since a bank will frequently pay more for $50,000 than $5,000. The trick is to report it to the IRS so that one person doesn't get saddled with the entire tax burden! We'll walk you through the proper tax-reporting process.

Can you earn too much interest? Although it's pleasant to see your net worth increase from interest earnings, realize that tax liabilities can also be increasing. Such increases can force you to file estimated tax papers on both state and federal levels. On the other hand, some deposit instruments (i.e., Treasury Bills) can be your ticket to tax-free interest earnings.

Everyone seems to be playing the banking game these days. Even major department stores are trying for center field! But the two main competitors are still banks and S&Ls. Although recent legislation has eliminated many of the differences, these institutions still have unique personalities. We'll highlight their differences and similarities and how they affect the average investor.

How safe is your money when deposited in a bank? Nightmares of the Great Depression still haunt America's big, average, and small investors. Any financial institution can fail — even the oldest and the best. By following the simple guidelines we've outlined, however, your risks can be negligible.

As we stated earlier, it's hard to avoid banks. They have become sophisticated institutions demanding a better educated consumer than ever before. Substantial profits and losses can be realized over a period of time depending on how you bank. With the help of our book, hopefully you too can number among those better equipped to meet the financial challenges of the 80s. It's your money, so learn how to use it to the best advantage possible!

Checking Accounts

R emember when you opened a checking account just so you could pay the bills? You probably only kept enough money in it to meet expenses and escape service fees.

Checking accounts aren't so simple anymore.

People have traditionally viewed checking accounts — also known as "demand deposit accounts" (DDA) — as a means to withdraw money on demand. Without prior notice, you can demand the withdrawal of any amount up to the balance of your account. In addition, you can close an account at any time without incurring penalties under federal law. (Banks can, however, incorporate into their service fee structures a charge for closing one within so many days of opening it.)

Remember Aunt Faye and how she didn't trust getting her money on demand from a savings account, so she kept $60,000 in plain old checking?

Every family had at least one Aunt Faye. Checking accounts were once a banker's gold mine, especially when people allowed large sums to remain on deposit for months or years.

How times have changed!

Modern-day banks still offer regular checking accounts which pay 0% interest and afford unlimited check-writing capability. In addition, they offer numerous other plans listed under the guise of checking services. Money can be accessed on demand through check-writing, and usually, through Automated Teller Machines (ATMs), and monthly statements are rendered. But oh boy are those interest rates ever different from Aunt Faye's 0% yield!

Of course, to use an old saying — "there are no free rides in life."

Not everyone is suited to every type of checking account. Choosing an account is rather like shopping for clothes. Different styles and sizes are available to meet individual needs. Of course, everyone can buy the exact same article, but won't most people look silly?

Well, "silly" may be too strong of a term for picking the wrong checking account, but our point is that individual needs are a major consideration when determining which plan can best meet your needs. Many people find it desirable to have more than one checking account — perhaps one for paying bills and another for investment purposes.

Today they can earn anywhere from 0% interest to double-digit interest rates. That's a pretty wide gap.

So why doesn't everyone simply ask for the highest yielding account and be done with the matter?

The answer can basically be found in those famous words we mentioned earlier — "there are no free rides in life."

True you can make a fair amount of interest on certain types of checking accounts, but anytime interest is involved there are strings attached.

Higher yielding accounts usually demand larger balances. Face it, one way banks attract large deposits is by sweetening the pot a bit. Some encourage account growth by varying the rate according to average balance for the month. The same account may be capable of earning many different rates depending on the balance involved. This is usually referred to as a "tiered" account.

Before we give you a rundown on some of the basic types of plans available, let's highlight some of the major considerations which generally come into play.

Balance — It's how much money you have in the account, correct? Yes, but in the world of banking that description is a little too vague. Banks recognize different types of balances. For example, the average balance and the balance as of statement day will probably be different. When shopping around for a checking account, make sure you understand balance re-strictions.

Let's say XYZ Bank offers 7% daily compounding on one type of checking account. One consideration may be that on statement day the account must have a balance of $2,500; otherwise, 0% interest will be earned. Even if a $50,000 balance is maintained every other day of the month, if the balance goes to $2,499 on statement day then $0 interest will be credited.

Minimum Deposit — Minimum deposit and balance may seem like interchangeable terms to the untrained eye. But they really aren't. In order to open some account types, you must make a minimum deposit. Most plans earning higher interest rates require an initial deposit of at least $1,000. Subsequent deposits may also have minimum restrictions, such as $100.

Banks sometimes offer what can be described as "cadillac accounts." Extremely high rates are paid along with such "bells-and-whistles" as free checks. What's the catch? Usually large minimums — perhaps $20,000 or more.

Access — Open a checking account and you have unlimited check writing capability as long as funds are available, right? Well it depends on what type of checking account you're dealing with. Some limit you to three checks per month.

Access restrictions are not always controlled by bank policy, but by law in some instances. Although deregulation has substantially loosened legal requirements, some federal regulations still apply. More about access restrictions will be discussed as we explain the various types of accounts available.

Overdraft Protection — Overdraft protection is a nice way of allowing you to write checks which would otherwise "bounce." For example, if you write a check for $250, but only $50 is available, overdraft protection provides for the $200 to be transferred from a designated account. Credit card accounts (i.e., MasterCard, Visa), savings accounts and other checking accounts are examples of popular sources for funds to cover overdrafts.

Automatic Transfer Services — We've devoted an entire chapter to the business of automatic transfer services. For the present, however, it's sufficient to say money can usually be transferred from one account to another on a regularly scheduled basis. Different from overdraft protection, transfer services are aimed at streamlining periodic deposits and payments by performing them automatically for customers.

Service Fees — What determines a service fee and how much it is varies depending on the bank. A service fee is usually calculated for each checking cycle (the days elapsing between statement days — usually one month). The number of checks written, the number of withdrawals made via ATMs, automatically transferred deposits, average balance, the frequency of using overdraft protection, etc. can affect service fee calculations. A bank can even assess a fee for maintaining the account.

If the bank is getting your money interest free (such as in the case of regular checking), why should they charge service fees?

It costs a bank money for every deposit and withdrawal made. Costs for processing a check are estimated to range from ten to thirty cents with expenses increasing yearly. Service fees help offset such expenses. The remainder is covered by the interest banks earn loaning out your money. The smaller the balance you maintain, the less profit a bank reaps. Face it, the guy who keeps a $50 average balance and writes 20 checks per month isn't exactly a profitable customer in the eyes of a banker! Thus, you have service fees.

Obviously we can't explain *your* bank's service fee calculations. Not only do banks differ, but their fees also vary depending on what type of account is involved. We can tell you, however, to be AWARE. Find out how much a fee can be and what determines it. Furthermore, realize service fees can and do change from time to time. Competition, changes in the law, and the introduction of new accounts typically motivate such changes.

"Extras" — "Money isn't the only thing in life!"
Bankers often subscribe to such a philosophy when it comes to enticing new customers. Offering free safe deposit boxes, reduced loan rates, free checks, etc. is one way some institutions compete. How about a shiny new cheese slicer?

"Extras" are great as long as rates and service fees remain competitive. But, who wants a cheese slicer if the rates are 1% less than the bank down the street? It's cheaper to buy the "extra" at the local discount store.

Such banks are nice, but don't let them blind you.

Checking accounts can create a need for bank-rendered services beyond the scope of normal customer support. Some of these services are listed below, along with sample fees:

Statement provided on other than the
    normal statement date .... $ 3.00

Accounts closed within 60 days of
    opening date .... $ 3.00

Checks returned for insufficient funds,
uncollected funds or post-dated $15.00

Deposited check which is dishonored and
returned unpaid and then subsequently
charged back to the account in which
it was deposited .... $ 3.00

Check certification .... $ 5.00

Stop payment order .... $ 8.00

Check which overdraws account $12.50

Photocopy of statement .... $ .50

Why do people have checking accounts?

Traditionally, checking accounts provided people with a means to exchange funds without actually handling money. Checks offer several advantages over currency:

1. Safer than carrying cash. If they are lost, stop payments can be placed on the missing checks.
2. Personal bookkeeping is streamlined. Paid checks provide a trail of how much money is spent where. Along with helping to balance the household budget, better records are available for tax purposes.
3. Money can safely be sent great distances. When mailing payments, it's safer to send a check than to stuff an envelope with money. Paid checks provide proof that such payments were received.
4. Large purchases can be made. People often want to spend more money than they have in their billfolds. Checking accounts allow them to access additional funds.

Of course there are other reasons why people have checking accounts. Some people simply want to establish a relationship with a bank in case of future credit needs. Individual requirements naturally come into play anytime people are managing their finances.

Modern-day banking has added quite a bit of spice to the once humdrum world of checking. People are discovering that checking accounts can be ideal vehicles for putting their money to work earning interest.

Opening a checking account nowadays is an investment.

Read the above sentence again. Think about it. Then ask yourself whether you number among the millions who still believe checking accounts are just for writing checks.

If your answer is "yes," then you're definitely in for an eye opening experience.

Regular — In spite of our promise to show you how checking accounts can boost interest earnings, we decided to start with the regular checking account. It's the granddaddy of them all!

Still the most popular type, 0% interest is earned. Applicable service fees are more lenient. There are no balance requirements. (Balances can, however, affect service fees.) Any number of checks can be written for sums as small or as big as you like.

NOW — Ever wonder what NOW stands for?

It's an acronym for "negotiated order of withdrawal." (We bet you're happier to stick with the abbreviation!)

NOW accounts were the first alternative to regular checking. Deregulation rulings effective January 1, 1986, removed interest ceilings for these accounts. Banks may now pay any rate they wish.

Many aspects of NOW and regular accounts are alike. Both permit you to write any number of checks for any amount. There are no legal restrictions as to minimum or maximum service fees. Although balances can impact service fees, there are no legal requirements.

If NOW and regular accounts are so similar, doesn't it make sense to go for the former since it pays interest?

Not necessarily. Higher minimum balances or higher transactional charges are usually assessed on NOW accounts.

With the introduction of some other accounts which we'll shortly discuss, NOWs have lost much of their appeal. They are, however, one way to earn interest on a checking account if you cannot meet the balance requirements demanded by other interest-bearing checking plans.

If you're interested in NOWs, just make sure monthly charges don't exceed interest earned.

MMIC — MMIC stands for Money Market Investment Checking. From a regulatory viewpoint, these accounts are also referred to as money market deposit accounts.

The concept of money market accounts originated in brokerage houses. A true "money market" account is a mutual fund similar to a stock market mutual fund. When you invest in the latter, your money is used to purchase stocks or bonds. Funds placed in a broker's money market account are lent for short periods to the U.S. Treasury, banks, companies, and sometimes foreign governments. The interest collected on such loans is then paid out as "dividends" to everyone who has invested in the fund. Both deposits and withdrawals are usually allowed on customer demand, although minimum requirements may exist.

Broker-controlled accounts are regulated by the Securities and Exchange Commission. They *are not* insured by either the FDIC or FSLIC (more about this particular topic in Chapter 16 —*Insurance — How Important Is It?*).

Although they take their name from that popular product marketed by brokers everywhere, MMIC accounts *are very different.*

First of all, if your bank is insured by the FDIC then any money deposited is insured up to the legal limit (presently $100,000). To make their profit which, in turn, allows them to pay you interest, this money becomes part of the bank's assets. Like money deposited in any other checking account, these funds assist in the making of home loans, business loans, car loans, etc.

Banks are not required to pay any specific interest rate. However, they must post for public view the rate they intend to pay. Such rates can and usually do change monthly.

How do banks determine these rates?

When MMIC accounts were introduced in December 1982, banks typically promoted them by offering very high rates. The goal was to attract money which had made its way into broker's money market funds. These promotions were very successful. Along with excellent rates, banks offered safety. Several billions in deposits were attracted. Now banks tend to pay what they think they must to remain competitive.

Banks often have a multi-tier system for setting rates. For example, a $20,000 account may earn a higher rate than a $5,000 one. Anyone can open an MMIC account (i.e., individuals, corporations, non-profit organizations).

MMICs no longer have a minimum balance requirement. Prior

to January 1, 1986, Federal law required that you keep a balance of $1,000 in order to earn the posted rate. That meant you needed at least $1,000 to open such an account. Today, minimum balance requirements like interest rates are controlled by bank policy rather than regulation.

Usually when MMICs are involved, banks still set a higher minimum balance requirement for them than other checking products. For example, if your balance falls below $1,000, the interest rate paid may not exceed 5.25% or perhaps even 0% will be earned. Interest rates and minimum balance requirements may be areas of competition for your neighborhood banks. By paying a little attention to the ads, you can earn extra dollars for your account.

Minimum requirements may also apply to deposits. Some banks demand deposits of at least $100. In this case, no legal restrictions apply — it is entirely bank policy.

Access to MMICs is limited to six preauthorized, automatic, telephone, or other third party transactions per month. Only three of these transactions can be by check. This is a federal regulation. Bank policy, however, does not usually dictate any minimum or maximum guidelines as to the size of each check. In addition, many banks permit you to transfer funds to a regular checking account, typically via ATMs. Another way to circumvent this regulatory restriction is simply to stop by a teller window and make a withdrawal.

As to service fees, banks may choose to assess them regardless of account balance or activity. Such philosophy is based partly on the fact that higher rates are paid; therefore, increasing costs make it necessary to charge some of the bank's maintenance upkeep to the customer.

When opening MMIC accounts, customers frequently won't even bother to order checks. As their name implies, these accounts are basically used as "investment" instruments. More like savings accounts than traditional checking accounts, MMICs are an excellent way to earn better than average interest rates yet have access to such funds on demand.

MM or SuperNOW — The MM stands for Money Market. These accounts are sort of a cross between NOWs and MMICs.

Like the MMIC, they too were tailored after the broker's money market accounts.

Introduced in January 1983, since "day 1" interest rates attributed to these accounts have traditionally been lower than those offered with MMICs. Like the MMIC, banks can have a multi-tier system for establishing rates. The only requirement is that rates must be posted for public view.

Federal law no longer dictates a minimum balance requirement of $1,000 in order to earn more than 5.25%. Prior to January 1, 1986, anytime the balance fell below $1,000, the interest rate had to revert to 5.25% or less.

Now let's pose an interesting question.

If the minimum balance requirements for MMICs and Super-NOWs are identical but the latter pay a lower rate, why would anyone want to open a SuperNOW?

A SuperNOW is more of a transactional account than what an MMIC is. There are no access limitations. Any number of deposits or withdrawals can be made per month.

There are restrictions, however, as to who can open one. Only an individual or a non-profit organization can open a Super-NOW. A business (i.e., corporation, partnership) *cannot* establish this type of account.

Because these accounts will accommodate any number of transactions, service fees for SuperNOWs are usually higher than those assessed for MMICs. However, there is presently a growing movement in the banking industry to reduce or even eliminate service fees connected with these checking accounts. SuperNOWs are especially attractive to people who maintain substantial balances yet have a need to write numerous checks each month.

Since interest rate ceilings and minimum balance requirements have been eliminated for all interest-bearing checking plans, there is a growing trend in the banking industry to restructure checking product lines. Many analysts predict that banks will gradually eliminate NOWs and SuperNOWs, replacing them with a single interest-paying checking account.

As we said earlier, many banks offer numerous checking plans. All plans, however, are actually variations of one of the above types. For example, XYZ Bank may offer a "Golden Investment Account" which requires a minimum balance of $50,000 and pays 10% interest compounded daily. Under regulatory classifications, the "Golden Investment Account" may actually be an MMIC account. If so, then MMIC access restrictions apply.

Our point is that banks can be as creative as they like when dreaming up checking accounts, but they must fall within one of the above categories when it comes to legal considerations.

Although deregulation has definitely loosened up the banking industry, it's still not a "free-for-all" business!

The days of plain old vanilla checking are gone. Deregulation is helping the banking industry to become a highly competitive and creative business. For the average consumer, comparison shopping is gaining momentum.

Today's interest rates are influenced by competition, short-term U.S. Securities, and Fed Funds. The latter are overnight investments between banks. In other words, banks can borrow from one another.

What interest rate is being paid? How is the interest compounded? Are there minimum deposit requirements? What are service fee calculations based on?

Picking the ideal checking account can demand some research on your part. More than one type of account may be needed. In the future, we expect to see even more variety in checking plans.

We also anticipate hearing more about truncation. The latter involves not returning customer's checks as part of the monthly statement rendering process. Copies could only be obtained on special request with an accompanying charge. Truncation is expected to have a major impact on service fees.

Another exciting area gaining ground in the world of checking involves point-of-sales (POS) processing. Already available on a limited basis, customers are supplied with plastic cards, similar to credit cards, which enable merchants to access their checking accounts. The sale amount is automatically deducted from the customer's checking account and then credited to the merchant's account.

Are you age 65 or older?

Giving a break to senior citizens is another popular "plus" offered by a growing number of banks. The Senior Citizen Account is usually a regular checking account available to customers age 65 years or older. Along with the age requirement, however, there's often another condition attached to these accounts in order for consumers to actually beat service fees. You may have to be on direct deposit for Social Security payments. Direct deposit assures the bank that a monthly deposit will be made to your account to cover checks being written. We'll talk more about these automatic deposits in Chapter 8 — *What's Direct Deposit?*.

Keep in mind that regardless of which checking plan you choose, they all share some handy features you need to know about.

At some time, you probably have seen the term "stop payment." Perhaps you've noticed it while reviewing a bank's service fees schedule, since usage of this service typically results in a fee to the customer.

"Stop payment" means that a customer has the privilege of stopping payment on any checks he has written, for whatever reason. By stopping payment, the customer is authorizing the bank to return his check to him even though money exists in the account for payment of the item.

Holds can be placed on accounts. One common example of a hold is "to watch customer signature," which you would use if you'd lost some checks and were concerned about someone forging your name.

There are times when only a "certified check" is acceptable. The checks you write day in and day out are commonly referred to as "personal checks." A certified check is typically used when the credit of the person writing it has not been established and the payee requires assurance that the funds are definitely on deposit at the bank. When obtaining a certified check, you usually write the bank a personal check for the amount involved plus a service fee. The bank will then issue you an official bank check with the word "certified" stamped on it. The funds are immediately withdrawn from your account.

Do you have trouble balancing your checkbook when statement time rolls around each month?

Most banks offer a checkbook reconciliation service. In other words, staff personnel will balance the statement for you. A fairly large fee is normally assessed. Although it may be available, we don't particularly recommend that you subscribe to this service. We feel it's good business if you personally keep on top of your own financial interests. And, with proper recordkeeping, it's easy to keep track of a checking account. Regardless of the checking plan involved, always obtain a check register and then it's easy to record all deposits and withdrawals.

Chapter 2

Savings Accounts

How bankers love those "passbook" savings accounts! Up until April 1, 1986, under federal regulation the maximum interest rate allowed was 5.5%. Savings accounts are cheaper for banks to support than other investment plans such as SuperNOWs. Remember how we said it presently costs a bank roughly 10 to 30 cents for every deposit or withdrawal made? Savings accounts usually experience little transactional activity when compared with most checking plans. Monthly statements are not always necessary. (Federal regulations, however, do require banks to render statements within so many days if ATM or direct deposit activity occurs. Otherwise, a bank is only required to issue statements annually.)

But from a customer viewpoint, are savings accounts really so wonderful?

No.

Americans keep more than $300 billion in savings accounts. Let's say banks are paying an average of 5.25% for this money. That represents an annual interest expense of around $15.75 billion. On the other hand, MMICs will probably pay an average of 7.5% Apply that rate to $300 billion and you get $22.5 billion. A $6.75 billion difference is a pretty nifty sum! No wonder bankers love savings accounts!

A savings account, in a fairly healthy interest market, will earn approximately 2% less than a comparable checking account. In terms of dollars and cents that means if you're keeping $25,000 in a savings account rather than a higher yielding checking account, then you're losing approximately $500 annually. Besides taking a significant hit on interest earnings, technically you might not be able to withdraw your money on demand.

Another name for checking accounts is demand deposit accounts. Those inside the financial community also have another name for savings accounts — time deposit accounts. Unlike checking accounts, where you have the right to withdraw your entire balance at any time during banking hours, you may have to give advance notice to make a withdrawal from your savings account. Banks have the legal right to require advance notice of withdrawals from such accounts, but in practice they rarely do. Even if you request a withdrawal of several thousand dollars, you can usually depend on receiving it immediately.

If savings accounts don't pay the best rates and can legally require you to give advance notice prior to making withdrawals, why do Americans keep more than $300 billion in them?

Depositing money in a savings account is practically a tradition. People are used to them. Until recently, there were only a limited number of ways you could deposit money in a bank. Regular checking and savings accounts were just about all the average investor ever came in contact with.

Most people don't understand many of the products offered by today's banks. They don't feel safe "experimenting with the unknown." The "unknown" is exactly how millions of people regard today's money market accounts with their multi-tier interest rate schedules and minimum balance requirements.

We *do not* mean to imply, however, that savings accounts are totally obsolete. They're a great way to teach children how to bank. If you can't meet the minimum balance required by money market accounts, a savings account may be your best bet since it's less tempting to withdraw money from the latter. Face it, checks can make withdrawing money a little too easy if you're lax in the self-restraint department. And no matter what we say, you still might be unwilling to switch funds to other types of investment accounts simply because of personal preferences.

If you choose to maintain a savings account, several factors should be considered.

Compounding — Any time you're investing money, it's important to understand what type of compounding period is being used. In fact, there's so much public confusion on this particular topic that we're devoting an entire chapter to the subject —Chapter 12 — *The Compounding & Interest Game*.

Aggressive marketing programs adopted by banks in most

major cities tend to accomplish two things when compounding is involved:

1. Emphasize when interest is paid and how it is compounded.
2. Keep compounding frequency to a competitive level. If the bank on West Street compounds daily and the one on East Street compounds monthly, with the right marketing campaign the former could steal the latter's customers.

Savings accounts, however, don't attract aggressive marketing campaigns. Think about it. When was the last time you saw or heard a bank ad dedicated to savings accounts.

We'd be willing to bet it was several years ago.

Because such accounts aren't publicly promoted, bankers may be a little more lax in staying competitive. If no one's talking about compounding or using it as a competitive edge, why bother to keep up with West Street Bank?

Savings accounts offer less than great interest rates anyhow, so don't lose any more money than you have to by getting saddled with a poor compounding plan.

Interest (360 or 365?) — How many days go into the calculation of your interest is another topic often ignored by people. Daily interest and daily compounding aren't the same. Unfortunately, many people believe they are. Because there is such a widespread misconception, we've chosen to elaborate on both these subjects in Chapter 12 — *The Compounding & Interest Game.*

In brief, daily interest means that you're going to earn interest every day your money is deposited in the account. If there are 31 days in a month, you'll earn 31 days of interest. On the other hand, if a bank pays monthly interest and bases such calculations on a 360 day year (yes, they can legally do that!), you'll earn only 30 days of interest each month.

The interest base is another feature that often suffers when there's no great competitive war waging among neighborhood banks. With some simple queries, however, you can discover what sort of timetables are being used. It's your money, so don't be afraid to ask questions. Shop around for the best deal in town.

Interest Crediting Date — The days of the month that you deposit and withdraw money from a savings account can affect the amount of interest credited.

For example, a deposit made during one month may not begin earning interest until the first day of the following month. On the other hand, a deposit made anytime during the first ten days of a month may earn interest as if it had been deposited on the first day of the month.

Although they do still exist, differences between interest crediting and actual transaction dates are not nearly as widespread as they were 10 or 15 years ago. Today most banks begin interest crediting calculations the same day a deposit or withdrawal is made.

Minimum Balance — Generally there is no minimum balance requirement, but don't take it for granted. Banks *can* stop paying interest when your balance falls below a certain amount. By the way, this minimum varies among banks and is ruled by policy rather than federal regulation.

Service Fees — Although most people don't associate service fees with savings accounts, banks are within their legal bounds to assess them. For example, along with ceasing interest payments once your balance falls below a specified amount the bank might just tack on a monthly service charge.

The main reason why we listed the above considerations was to emphasize that not all savings plans are created equal. Although savings accounts are still somewhat regulated by the federal government (that's why interest rates were limited until recently), banks have some flexibility in designing them. As we continue exploring other investment options (i.e., CDs, IRAs), we'll often remind you that regulation doesn't govern every single aspect of most investment plans. The trick is to learn what you're shopping for and how to determine who's got the best deal in town.

If savings accounts are the investment plan you're shopping for, banks usually have more than one type for you to choose from. The following are highlights of the basic types you'll find nationwide.

Regular —Sometimes called "passbook" accounts because, for years, customers were issued actual passbooks. Every time a deposit or withdrawal was made, the transaction was noted in the passbook by special machines located at teller windows. Prior to machines, manual entries were made by authorized bank personnel. When interest was due to be paid, customers had to bring their passbooks into the bank and have them updated with the appropriate credit.

Among the sweeping changes computerization has made in the banking industry is the virtual elimination of passbooks. Customer statements have replaced them in most banks throughout the United States. All deposits, withdrawals, and interest payments are usually recapped in statement form nowadays. But *how often* statements are mailed to customers depends largely on bank policy. Federal regulations do demand at least one statement per year be rendered. As we mentioned earlier, ATM and direct deposit activity can require more frequent issuance.

Why does ATM and direct deposit activity demand special treatment?

The federal government feels it's important for customers to be aware of any electronic activity involving their accounts before a long period of time has elapsed. Unauthorized electronic activity is indeed a topic of growing concern for bankers and government officials alike. Affording customers with frequent monitoring capability is one way regulatory agencies are helping to curb long-term unauthorized usage.

For example, ATM activity requires you to use a plastic card electronically encoded with data pertinent to access a customer's account through an Automated Teller Machine. These cards can be stolen and the code potentially broken. Some people even aid the thief by writing their password on the card itself. Banks are required to issue a monthly statement when an account has experienced ATM activity. This allows the customer to be notified of any such transactions within 30 days of occurrence. Regulation E also stipulates that customers must be furnished with a description of where such transactions occur.

Example:

04/30/85	$20.00	ATM WITHDRAWAL
		XYZ MALL, NEW YORK, NY

Regular accounts are by far the most popular savings type. A minimum balance is rarely required. In addition, there is generally no limit on the size and number of transactions made each month.

TDOA — Time deposit open accounts (sometimes called open-time savings accounts) involve the customer agreeing to make deposits to his account for a given period of time, with a penalty being assessed for early withdrawals. With this type of savings plan, withdrawals are penalty-free during the first 10 days of each deposit term. Until January 1 1986, withdrawals after the 10-day period were penalized as required by Regulation Q. As you can see, penalty calculations change from time to time due to regulatory revisions. Banks can also assess their own penalties for early withdrawals in addition to those specified by law, thus penalties may still be in effect regardless of deregulation.

When these accounts were initially introduced, they appealed to the more sophisticated depositor. Large amounts of money could be invested at higher rates than offered by regular accounts.

Today, TDOAs have little appeal to the smart investor. Better rates can almost always be obtained by investing in money market checking plans, CDs, U.S. Securities, etc. In addition, plans such as MMICs eliminate the risk of penalty for early withdrawals. However, with deregulation eliminating TDOA interest rate ceilings and penalties it might be wise to keep your eyes and ears open for any new products introduced by banks. There is speculation that some creative bankers might be designing a new breed of TDOA products.

Christmas Club — In spite of the low interest they typically pay, Christmas Clubs are still popular. Designed to help people save for holiday spending sprees, customers deposit the same amount each week.

Clubs come in different amounts. There are $1, $5, $10, $20, etc. clubs. Since regular deposits for identical amounts are required, banks frequently offer customers the ability to authorize the automatic transfer of such funds from checking accounts. More about this service in Chapter 9 — *Automatic Transfer Services.*

Rather than paying interest, some clubs will automatically credit your account with the last payment. Christmas Club checks are usually issued several weeks prior to Christmas. These accounts must be opened new each year. Their main advantage is to encourage people to set aside funds for the holiday season by scheduling regular deposits. By setting aside a few dollars each week, a nice holiday nest egg can be accumulated.

When shopping around for a club, we recommend you consider the following:

1. Interest rate paid.
2. How interest is compounded.
3. Can deposits be automatically credited. Thanks to direct deposit, no longer must your checking account be located at the same bank.
4. "Extras!"

What on earth do we mean by "extras?"

Bankers frequently offer a gift when you open a Christmas Club. Candles, ornaments, serving trays, and bibles are popular examples. If interest and convenience are comparable, why not let the gift be the tie breaker if it appeals to you? There's nothing wrong with that. In fact, that's why bankers offer them — to get that competitive edge.

Vacation Club — As the name implies, a Vacation Club was designed to help you save for a vacation. Less popular than its Christmas Club counterpart, Vacation Clubs are usually offered only by larger banks.

Essentially, they operate the same as Christmas Clubs. Checks are issued at the beginning of summer. Deposits can probably be pre-authorized and handled automatically. New clubs must be opened yearly.

If you go shopping for a Vacation Club, you probably won't have many to choose from. If possible, though, the same considerations we recommend for selecting a Christmas Club apply.

Banks can design their own savings plan (i.e., Silver Savings, Home Repair Club). The only restriction is that they must adhere to regulatory requirements specified for the actual account type. For instance, Christmas, Vacation, and Home Repair are all, technically, club accounts. Furthermore, a club account actually fits in the regular or TDOA category depending on how it's designed. For example, when interest rate ceilings were still in effect, if your Christmas Club paid more than

5.5% it was really a TDOA subject to penalties for early with-drawals. Now, however, deregulation has eliminated much of the need to even bother with making such distinctions.

When it comes to savings accounts, our best tip is to take a long hard look at whether you should have one. For the most part, savings accounts are obsolete. Better interest rates and access freedom can be found in other bank products.

If they're so obsolete, why do banks still offer them?

Bankers like to make money. That's their business. They borrow from one and lend to another. Why should they encourage anyone to move money into higher paying accounts? Learning how to invest your money wisely is your job.

Find out what your bank and others have to offer in the way of interest-bearing accounts. Then ask yourself whether maintaining funds in a savings account is really a wise decision or simply a habit.

CDs

CD s is an acronym for Certificates of Deposit. When banks issue CDs, usual procedures include issuing the customer a formal statement or certificate. This form indicates that a named person(s) has on deposit a specified sum of money which may be withdrawn without penalty at the end of a stated period.

Another way to define a CD is to compare it to a contract. When you choose to purchase a CD, you're agreeing to lend your money to a bank under certain conditions. Conditions agreed upon between you and the bank generally include the amount, interest rate, compounding frequency, when the agreement will end (commonly referred to as the "maturity date"), when interest will be paid and whether the instrument is automatically renewable. The contract drawn up between you and your banker spell out these considerations. A copy is given to you and a-carbon retained for bank records. To withdraw money, the CD must be cashed in. If you withdraw only part of the money, a new CD must be drawn up because in keeping with our contract analogy, at least one condition of the agreement has changed —the amount.

For years CDs were issued only in large denominations (i.e. $1,000, $5,000, $10,000). The minimum maturity was generally six months. Penalties were assessed for early withdrawals. Interest rates, however, were usually higher then those paid for savings accounts. Banks could afford to pay higher rates because they had an assurance of keeping the money for the period set forth in the certificate. On the other hand, money housed in checking or savings accounts were much more subject to being withdrawn at any time.

Prior to October 1983 the federal government tightly regulated the CD market. Interest rates, minimum deposits and minimum length of deposit were conditions specified by the government.

Deregulation, as we've previously emphasized, has resulted in sweeping changes throughout the banking industry. From an investor's viewpoint, deregulation has made the CD market more attractive!

If you still have an FDIC or FSLIC insured CD issued prior to October 1983, the old regulatory rules apply. We recommend before doing anything with these instruments (besides holding them to maturity) that you read the fine print. Unfortunately many people purchased long-term CDs years ago and they are now locked into a low interest rates. If you're one of these unfortunates and wish to cash in your CD early, keep in mind that the old penalty rules apply. Along with a copy of your certificate, you should have been furnished with a form explaining penalties. Both government and bank-imposed penalties may be assessed.

Now let's take a look at how deregulation has changed the CD market.

CDs with maturity terms of 32 days or more are no longer subject to interest rate ceilings. In addition, minimum deposits are no longer regulated.

If you withdraw money prior to maturity, the government still requires banks to assess a penalty. On CDs for one year or less, the penalty is 31 day's interest. If the instrument is for one year or more, 90 days interest is taken as the penalty amount.

Okay, if the government isn't controlling the CD market, who or what determines such conditions as interest rates and minimum deposits.

The market determines most aspects of today's CDs.

Interest rates, maturity terms, compounding frequency and minimum deposits are controlled largely by how much banks want your money. If there are several financial institutions in your town and competition is fierce for depositors' dollars, then you're probably going to get better terms than if you live in a one bank town.

In larger cities, rate wars will occasionally break out. Usually all it takes to set one off is one or two financial institutions eager to expand their deposits.

What do rate wars mean to the average investor?

You'll probably have periodic opportunities to earn higher than usual rates. It may last for weeks or months.

What do "battles for dollars" mean to bank management?

Bankers tend to believe that once they get your money, you'll continue to leave it on deposit after the rate war is over. And they're usually right. Unfortunately, most people don't realize when the war is over. We use the term "unfortunate" because all

Blue Ridge Bank, NA
One Mountain Drive • Box 101
Park Hills, VA 25326

CERTIFICATE OF DEPOSIT

ORIGINAL

ISSUE DATE
October 12, 1985

INVESTMENT NUMBER
679052

THIS CERTIFIES THAT: John Doe
111 First Street
NoWhere, VA   00001

HAS DEPOSITED WITH THE BLUE RIDGE BANK, N.A. THE
SUM OF $10,000.00. THE BANK HEREBY AGREES TO REPAY
THIS SUM PLUS INTEREST AT THE RATE OF 10.20% PER
ANNUM 180 DAYS AFTER THE ISSUE DATE UPON SUR-
RENDER OF THE ORIGINAL CERTIFICATE PROPERLY
ENDORSED.

THIS CERTIFICATE IS AN AUTOMATICALLY RENEWABLE
INVESTMENT UNLESS OTHERWISE STATED BELOW.

THIS INVESTMENT CERTIFICATE IS ISSUED SUBJECT TO THE
TERMS AND CONDITIONS APPEARING ON THE REVERSE
SIDE HEREOF.

(MATURITY DATE: April 10, 1986)

BLUE RIDGE BANK, NA

BY _____
AUTHORIZED SIGNATURE

PAYABLE AT:
BLUE RIDGE BANK, NA
ONE MOUNTAIN DRIVE, BOX 101
PARK HILLS, VA 25326

NON—TRANSFERABLE
NON-NEGOTIABLE

Sample CD. (Front Side)

CERTIFICATE OF DEPOSIT TERMS AND CONDITIONS

If this is an automatically renewable certificate, it will be automatically renewed for successive terms equal to the original term unless presented for redemption on or within 5 days after the original or any subsequent maturity date. Blue Ridge Bank, N.A. reserves the right to redeem the certificate provided written notice is mailed to the owner, at the last known address, at least 30 days prior to the next maturity date. The interest rate on any automatic renewal of this certificate will be the maximum rate the Bank is paying at the maturity date or subsequent maturity dates on Certificates of Deposit of the same type and term. This rate will be within the limitations, if any, set by Federal Regulation.

In purchasing this certificate, you have agreed to keep these funds on deposit for a fixed period of time.

"Federal law and regulations prohibit the payment of a Time Deposit prior to maturity unless substantial interest is forfeited."

1. Where a Time Deposit with an original maturity of 32 days to one year, or any portion thereof, is paid before maturity, a depositor shall forfeit at least one (1) month of interest on the amount withdrawn at the rate being paid on the deposit. Even if the funds have been on deposit for less than one (1) month, the one (1) month interest penalty shall apply and will be deducted from the principal.

2. Where a Time Deposit with an original maturity of more than one (1) year, or any portion thereof, is paid before maturity, a depositor shall forfeit at least three (3) months of interest on the amount withdrawn at the rate being paid on the deposit. Even if the funds have been on deposit for less than three (3) months, the three (3) months interest penalty shall apply and will be deducted from the principal.

All agreements relating to this certificate shall be subject to change without notice insofar as it may be necessary for the Bank to comply with any law or regulations enacted or promulgated by competent federal or state authority.

Sample CD. (Back Side)

too often the winner of rate wars will end up offering less competitive terms once the battle is over. Our advice is to keep track of who's paying what regardless of whether your town is in the midst of a rate war.

If you're going to go shopping for a CD, then you've got to understand what to look for.

Minimum Deposit — Isn't it strange how banks never mention maximum deposits? It's probably because the more you deposit, the happier they are!

Minimum deposits and interest rates, however, often are related. The average minimum for most maturities is presently $500. Higher rates, especially for short term instruments, usually demand substantial minimums.

For example, XYZ Bank may market what they call a "Golden Certificate." Let's say it has a 1-year maturity and pays 12% interest compounded quarterly. In today's market that's one sweet deal! One-year instruments have been averaging between 6.25– 7.00% compounded annually. So what's the catch? That "Golden Certificate" requires a minimum deposit of $25,000.

Interest Rate — Interest rates typically simulate yields on U.S. Treasury bills and notes. Of course market conditions in your town can change this commonly used index. Rate wars are one example. Another example is simply a lack of competition.

Generally the longer you agree to leave your money on deposit, the higher the rate. This is because banks are guaranteed having these dollars for extended periods of time and thus can make longer term investments with such funds.

Most CDs are fixed-rate instruments. This means they pay the same interest rate throughout their term. If it's a 7-year instrument at 8% compounded annually, you'll earn 8% simple interest for 7 years.

Variable-rate instruments may also be available in your area. Variable-rate CDs are usually not as popular with financial institutions or the general public. With these instruments, interest rates change according to market conditions. For example, the rate may be adjusted monthly according to what newly issued 6-month T-bills are earning.

Compounding Frequency — Compounding frequency is a characteristic of investment accounts we've consistently attempted to emphasize. Why? Basically because it's one of the most ignored and least understood aspects of the investment business. Hopefully by the time you finish *Chapter 12 — The Compounding & Interest Game* you'll be a pro at deciphering such terminology as "7% daily interest compounded monthly."

For the present, we want to emphasize the importance of exploring what a CD's *effective annual yield* is. The rate a bank pays and the rate you actually earn can be different. In other words, 7% interest doesn't necessarily mean you'll earn 7%. Compounding affects the rate you actually earn. Disclosure of the "effective annual yield" takes compounding into consideration.

Let's say Main Street Bank compounds interest quarterly on your CD. In simple language, this means Main Street Bank takes the interest you earn each quarter and adds it to the principal. From then on, you're earning interest on a higher balance. Each quarter it increments by the amount of your new quarterly interest earnings. Thus, your yield goes up. Our advice is to ask around and compare effective annual yields.

EFFECTIVE ANNUAL YIELDS OF CDs PAYING:

Compounded	6%	7%	8%	9%	10%	11%
annually	6.000	7.000	8.000	9.000	10.000	11.000
quarterly	6.136	7.186	8.243	9.308	10.381	11.462
monthly	6.168	7.229	8.300	9.381	10.471	11.572
weekly	6.180	7.246	8.322	9.409	10.507	11.615
daily	6.183	7.250	8.328	9.416	10.516	11.626

Maturity — Remember how we compared a certificate to a contract?

Contracts usually end when all obligations have been met. Likewise the life of a certificate is stipulated as part of the contractual agreement you make when purchasing a CD. At some point in the future, you and the bank mutually agree that the CD "matures" and that funds can be withdrawn without incurring penalties.

The day you buy a CD is referred to as the "purchase date."

The day your CD can be redeemed is referred to as the "maturity date."

Naturally, terms affect maturity dates. In today's deregulated market, you actually can buy CDs maturing on specific days if so desired. The only stipulation is that the term must be at least 32 days. For example, you may have some money to invest but need it available in time to pay your taxes on April 15. If you choose to invest these funds in a CD, you could ask for a maturity date of April 15 (providing it's at least 32 days in the future).

Terms and maturities are at your discretion, as long as they are within reason. (It's highly unlikely any bank will sell you a CD that matures in 50 years!). The certificate life you desire depends on such factors as how long you can afford to invest funds, the rate you're seeking, and anticipated market conditions.

If you cash in a CD prior to its maturity date, you will incur government-imposed penalties. Regulations still rule when early withdrawals are involved.

When shopping for maturities and the rates they bring, realize that banks usually post in their lobbies interest rates and corresponding terms. In addition, many support a telephone number you can dial for a recap of current rates and maturities.

SAMPLE RATE AND MATURITY SCHEDULE

CD Rate/Maturity Schedule effective 3-26-85 through 4-1-85

Term	Rate	Minimum Deposit	Interest Method
32–89 days	8.20	$500	simple
90–179 days	8.60	$500	simple
180–269 days	8.90	$500	simple
270–364 days	9.20	$500	simple
365 days but less than 2 yrs.	9.35	$500	simple
2 yrs. but less than 3 yrs.	9.75	$500	simple
3 yrs. but less than 4 yrs.	10.00	$500	simple
4 yrs. through 5 yrs.	10.25	$500	simple

Interest Frequency — Banks can and do differ in when they pay interest. An attractive interest frequency helps compensate for annual compounding (also referred to as simple interest).

If your CD pays interest monthly, interest payments can be deposited in an interest bearing checking account (i.e. Super-NOW, MMIC) or a savings account where additional earnings can be reaped.

Banks will often give you a choice as to when you want your interest paid (i.e. monthly, quarterly, annually, term). "Term" indicates that interest will be paid when the instrument matures. If you purchase a 3 year CD and choose interest payable at term, no interest will be paid until it matures (and that's 1,095 days down the road!) Unless you have a good compounding plan, such as daily or monthly, we recommend you opt for more frequent interest payments than term or annual. Interest earnings will then be yours to periodically invest or mix with the family budget for expenses. In fact, some people on fixed incomes purchase long-term CDs and request monthly interest payments as a means to supplement their incomes.

Renewable vs. Non-Renewable — As we've already established, CDs always have maturity dates. Once a certificate matures, you must determine whether it will be redeemed or renewed. When you redeem it, the deposit amount plus any interest due is paid. If it's renewed, a new maturity date is established.

There are two ways a CD can be renewed — manually or automatically.

When you purchase one of these instruments, it's customary for bank personnel to ask whether you want it to be "automatically renewable" or "non-renewable." If you opt for "automatically renewable," the bank will automatically re-invest your CD money in a like instrument when the maturity date is reached. All conditions pertinent to the original instrument will stay the same with the exception of interest rate. The latter is adjusted to agree with current rate policy. Generally a statement is mailed to you acknowledging that the money has been re-invested and at what interest rate.

Many people find the automatically renewable option a real time-saver; it eliminates having to stop by the bank every time a

CD matures. Furthermore, just because the automatically renewable option is selected doesn't mean you can't redeem it on maturity. In fact it will continue to renew until you eventually cash it in on a maturity date.

Non-renewable CDs can naturally be re-invested in like instruments. However, this must be handled manually by both the customer and bank personnel. A new certificate must be drawn up; thus, any conditions (not just the interest rate) can be changed (i.e., depositors' names, term, amount).

When shopping for a CD in today's deregulated market, it's fairly safe to say that almost anything goes. CDs can be written in a variety of ways, allowing banks to better meet individual needs. Flexible maturity terms is an especially attractive feature. While one person may be seeking a 5-year instrument affording monthly interest checks, perhaps another wishes to access to the principal every 3 months.

Although they may vary greatly in maturities, rates, and compounding frequencies, most CDs are classified by those inside the financial community as "regular certificates." Another instrument in the CD category is marketed on a much more limited basis. These instruments are called "original issue discount certificates" or "OIDs."

OIDs are written with terms greater than one year. Interest is paid at maturity. However, any interest earned during a year is reported to the IRS for income tax purposes. If early withdrawals are made, tax adjustments are usually required.

An OID is sold for less than its face value. For example, a $10,000 OID may be sold for $9,900. The $100 difference between discount amount and face amount is what you will earn if the OID is held to maturity.

Are CDs the right investment for everyone?

No. Like any investment option, CDs have both positive and negative aspects. True, you can usually earn higher rates by purchasing CDs rather than depositing money in MMICs, but access is limited. Generally the better the rate, the longer you must agree to leave funds on deposit.

Sometimes you can't afford to tie up funds for extended periods of time. Also, locking into a specific interest rate for several years is a gamble. If rates go up, you lose. If they go down, you're one smart cookie! A few years ago CDs were paying 15% and up. Considering how rates have tumbled, those who locked into 15% rates for 4 or 5 years were indeed the winners in today's money market game.

If CDs prove to be the ideal investment vehicle for you, you're probably going to discover that not all banks are alike when it comes to rates, effective annual yields, etc. You've heard of people shopping by mail? Along with flower seeds, cooking gadgets and clothing, CDs can be bought through the mail. As long as the issuing institution is insured by the FDIC or FSLIC, mail order CDs are as safe as any purchased in your hometown. If you're interested in some out-of-town shopping, just browse the ads in *The Wall Street Journal* or the Sunday *New York Times*. Some institutions even support toll-free 800 numbers for you to call concerning rates.

And last but certainly not least in the world of comparative CD shopping, don't be afraid to ask one financial institution to match what another is offering. You'll be amazed at how many will agree to such a demand, especially if otherwise it means losing a customer to their competitor across town.

Chapter 4

IRAs

The Individual Retirement Account, or IRA as it's commonly called, is one of today's hottest savings products.

Unless you are in that infamous "filthy rich" category, coping financially after retirement probably concerns you. Will Social Security be around in 30 years? If it is, will those monthly checks keep pace with inflation? Will funds from your company retirement plan be invested wisely? What if you never remain with one employer long enough to become vested? What if you're self-employed?

Investing in an IRA can be your ticket to a financially secure retirement. Anyone who has employment income can invest in one. IRAs are marketed throughout the United States by banks, S&Ls, brokerage houses, insurance companies, and credit unions. Since our goal is to help you put your money to work at the local bank, naturally we've placed special emphasis on what banks have to offer.

First, however, let's look at IRA plans in general. Any wage earner under 70½ years of age can open one. Regardless of whether you're already participating in other retirement programs (i.e., company pensions, Keoghs, profit sharing plans), you're still eligible. Benefits from other retirement plans, including Social Security, are not affected.

What does it mean "to make a contribution"?

Depositing money in an IRA is often referred to as "making a contribution." Eligible individuals can make annual contributions of $2,000 or 100% of the current year's earnings, whichever is less. In other words, if you worked part-time and earned $1,500 for the year, you could contribute the entire $1,500. Up those earnings to $2,000 and you can contribute $2,000. Earn $18,000 and $2,000 is still the most you can contribute.

If there are two wage earners in a family, two separate IRAs may be established. Each spouse can contribute $2,000; funds go to the individual accounts.

What if one spouse doesn't work?

Spousal IRAs are the answer. If your spouse does not have his or her own earned income, an additional $250 can be contributed, upping the maximum to $2,250. When a spousal account is involved, a specific portion of all IRA contributions must be set aside in each spouse's name. Let's say you make the maximum contribution — $2,250. The following are a few examples of valid splits:

Husband	Wife
$1,125	$1,125
$1,000	$1,125
$1,250	$1,000
$1,500	$ 750

Our point is that it's personal preference *how* you divide up IRA contributions when spousal accounts are involved.

How much do you have to contribute each year?

There are no minimums for regular or spousal accounts. Annual contributions can vary from zero to the maximum allowable under law. If funds are unavailable, it's legal to borrow money to invest in an IRA. However, it is *not* legal to use IRA funds as collateral for loans.

Does your entire annual contribution have to be made at one time?

No, contributions are made monthly, quarterly, annually, etc. Most IRA plans are flexible enough to accommodate whatever timetable best suits individual needs. For example, one participant may choose to contribute $500 each quarter whereas another participant may choose to contribute $100 each month. If you establish an IRA with a bank or S&L, these institutions may be able to make deposits for you automatically by transferring funds from other accounts such as checking.

Not only can IRA contributions be made anytime during the calendar year, but there's even some leeway into the next year. Accounts designated for the previous year can be opened or contributed to through your income tax filing date (April 15 unless extensions are involved). In other words, through April 15, 1987, you can make a 1986 contribution. As we'll soon discover, IRAs afford some definite tax breaks. By allowing contributions to be made after December 31, taxable income can be reduced after all income and deduction amounts are available. Such leeway allows extra time to determine whether an IRA contribution will help reduce Uncle Sam's present tax bite!

While you can legally contribute to an IRA any time from January 1 through April 15 of the following year (or longer with a filing extension), it pays not to procrastinate. The following table shows differences in accumulation based on contributing the first day of the year versus the last for an IRA yielding 10% annually. If interest rates or compounding frequencies are better, naturally the differences between start-of-year and end-of-year contributions become even greater.

RETIREMENT ACCUMULATION TABLE
(based on 10% annual interest)

Contribute	15 Years	20 Years	25 Years	30 Years
$2,000 the first of each year	$69,899	$126,005	$216,364	$361,889
$2,000 at end of each year	63,545	114,550	196,694	328,988
Additional accumulation through early contribution	$ 6,354	$ 11,455	$ 19,670	$ 32,901

When it comes to IRA contributions, there is one point we want to especially emphasize.

How much and when you contribute can vary from year to year. You are under no obligation to continue making deposits once you open an account.

Establishing an IRA is one way to insure income during retirement years. For most people, however, retirement is a long time off. So why bother to invest decades ahead of time?

The sooner you start saving money, the more you'll accumulate. That's obvious. Someone who invests $2,000 annually for 30 years will end up with a bigger nest egg than someone else who invests $1,000 for 20 years.

IRA PROJECTION TABLE
$2,000 Payment Made at the Start of Each Year
Accumulation at the end of . . .

Annual Rate	10 Years	15 Years	20 Years	25 Years
8%	$31,291	$ 58,649	$ 98,846	$157,909
10%	35,062	69,899	126,005	216,364
12%	39,309	83,507	161,397	298,668
14%	44,089	99,961	207,537	414,666
16%	49,466	119,850	267,681	578,177

What many people don't understand is how much can be saved through immediate tax credits. For every dollar invested in an IRA, an equal tax credit is reaped.

If you have a taxable income of $25,000 and contribute $2,000, your taxable income is reduced to $23,000. Married couples who are both wage earners can contribute and take a deduction of up to $2,000 each on a single tax return or up to $4,000 on a joint tax return. Individuals with non-wage earning spouses who establish a regular IRA and a spousal IRA can contribute and take a deduction of up to $2,250 on a joint tax return. Money invested in an IRA is deductible regardless of whether other deductions are itemized at tax reporting time.

So in summary, IRAs help you save two ways:
1. Money is set aside for retirement years.
2. Current taxable income is reduced.

The full amount you contribute to an IRA as well as the interest earned on your contributions accumulate free of current income tax until you begin making withdrawals. These withdrawals are commonly referred to as "distributions". As we'll shortly discover, age plays a major role in determining when withdrawals can begin without incurring penalties. One of the major benefits reaped from an IRA is the untaxed growth of deposits and interest until you are in a lower tax bracket.

If you withdraw funds from an IRA prior to reaching age 59½, you will incur penalties. In addition to ordinary income taxes, a 10% penalty is assessed on early withdrawals; exceptions will be granted only if death or disability occurs. Depending on how funds are invested, substantial interest penalties may be another costly consideration.

After age 59½, funds may be withdrawn without penalty. At that time, you can receive the entire amount of the IRA in one lump sum or receive periodic payments. Retirement years usually mean lower tax brackets; once IRA funds are taxed, less (if any) is lost through taxation.

IRA participants *must* begin withdrawing funds by no later than age 70½ or pay a 50% tax on the amount which the IRS feels should have been withdrawn. A formula has been developed to calculate the minimum amount a participant must withdraw. The formula is rather complicated and considers the participant's projected life span. The latter is derived from tables prepared by life insurance companies. Your IRA custodian (the institution that manages your account) can supply more specifics about this formula and how it relates to you personally.

When establishing an IRA, a beneficiary must be named. If the account holder dies prior to withdrawing any or all funds, the entire amount held in the account must be distributed to the named beneficiary within five years. However, the beneficiary may elect to treat this account as his or her own IRA. By "adopting" the IRA, the beneficiary may *potentially* escape all penalty and tax assessments. We emphasized the word "potentially" because the same provisions apply when a beneficiary assumes an IRA. In other words, if the beneficiary is under age 59½ and assumes the IRA then withdrawals cannot be made without paying penalties.

As we said earlier, IRAs are marketed by banks, insurance companies, brokerage houses, etc. Furthermore, anyone can change custodians. All you have to do is tell the present custodian where to send the money and pay any penalties specified in your IRA agreement. In this instance, the "penalties" we're talking about originate from company policy rather then federal regulation. Such fees can be substantial. They also vary depending on the institution involved.

Is there a limit to how many IRAs one person can establish?

No. Any number of IRAs can be opened. The only restriction is that total annual contributions cannot exceed the maximum allowable under law.

It's also legal to "roll over" an IRA once a year. "Roll over" means taking physical possession of the assets in an IRA. If you're ever in a financial bind, this may prove to be one handy feature! The only stipulation is that these assets must be placed in another IRA within 60 days; otherwise, income taxes along with a 10% penalty will be assessed.

The transfer of a lump-sum distribution from a qualified employer's plan to an IRA is also regarded as a roll-over contribution. Any lump-sum distribution from your employer's qualified pension plan can be rolled over into an IRA, but again this must occur within 60 days of the date distribution is received.

IRAs are famous for the numerous investment options they offer. Bank CDs, mutual funds, annuities, stocks, corporate bonds and government securities are examples of *how* IRA dollars may be invested. Furthermore, participants can convert their assets into different instruments. For example, funds from a matured CD may be re-invested in common stocks.

What about risks?

How much risk you take depends on which investment option(s) you choose.

Risk-free plans are available through most federally insured banks and S&Ls. Although only moderate growth will be realized, each participant is insured for $100,000 if FDIC or FSLIC coverage applies. Since this coverage applies new at each institution,establishing multiple IRAs at different banks or S&Ls can increase this valuable coverage. Just remember to keep each account at or below $100,000.

Not all banks, through, are equal when it comes to IRAs. Aggressive competition is often seen in the selling of this particular product. Interest rates and compounding frequencies are usually the main thrusts of such marketing strategies.

Banks rarely charge a fee to establish or maintain an IRA. However, most will charge you a fee for transferring the account to another custodian. Any such fees must be detailed in the IRA agreement you sign. Our best advice? Read the agreement before signing it and ask questions if you don't understand.

Almost all banks sell special IRA 18-month CD. These certificates earn whatever interest rate the bank is willing to pay. In other words, competition is a key factor in determining what a bank-managed IRA will yield.

Typically banks offer both fixed rate and variable rate plans. Under the fixed plan, the interest rate will change periodically (otherwise, you could stay at the same rate for 30 years!) but is guaranteed from deposit date to maturity date. Variable rate signifies that the rate can potentially go up and down over the life of the instrument.

Government regulations *do not* limit the type of savings plan that a bank can use as a vehicle for IRAs. Banks use MMICs, 18-month CDs, 5-year CDs, etc. In all cases, however, the same federal regulations apply to contributions and withdrawals.

Regardless of where you establish an IRA, a few words of caution about accumulation figures. When you look at a chart and see what could be earned in 20, 25 or 30 years, the amount shown seems very attractive. But what about inflation? If the future is anything like the past, inflation will definitely nibble away (devour may be a better term!) at your IRA money.

When analyzing retirement payouts from IRAs, the key is to consider future inflation. For a realistic view, you must adjust either the interest rate used or the purchasing power of future dollars due to be received. Economists indicate that over long periods of time interest rates average only about 3% more than inflation rates. So the next time you're dazed by an IRA accumulation chart, remember that $100,000 in 20 years probably won't begin to equal the purchasing power of $100,000 today.

Chapter 5

Discount Brokerage

B anking used to be simple. It was a business of borrowing from those who had money and lending to those who didn't. Rate differences between deposits and loans represented gross profits. Expenses were paid; stockholders received regular dividend checks.

Those days when the banking business was basically limited to cashing checks and making loans are gone forever. Today's banks, especially the larger ones, are also in the business of selling financial services. Bank economists observe that fee-related services will represent a significant share of the industry's future earnings, particularly since deregulation and more liberalized state laws are allowing banks to enter new territories.

Why is there such a move within the banking community to introduce products whose profit potentials rest more on fees than interest?

It's simple. Fees are stable; interest rates are often chaotic. Fees make it easier for bank management to guarantee profits. Shifting interest rates make it difficult to insure adequate profit margins.

Discount brokerage is one of the newest and most popular fee-based services offered by banks nationwide. As its name implies, "discount brokerage" involves the selling of a service similar to that offered by professional stockbrokers at a discounted price.

What's the keyword?

Discount! Bankers aren't the only people offering this service. Look in the telephone book of any major city and you should see listings for one or more independent discount brokers. However, since banking is the topic of our book, naturally we're going to concentrate on how banks approach this service.

Discount brokerage enables you to buy and sell stocks and bonds at very low, discounted commission rates by cutting out certain services offered by traditional brokerage houses. Fees charged by banks and brokerage houses can vary as much as 70%. Although the savings can be significant, discount brokerage isn't for everyone. It was designed for the independent-minded investor who prefers to make his or her own investment decisions.

You make the decisions.

Note how we emphasized the word "you."

Discount brokers usually don't give advice on what to buy and sell or when to do it. They save you money by focusing on essential services and eliminating a lot of the extras. For example, banks don't pay a sales force nor do they maintain a research department. Of course one obvious advantage is that there are no sales people high-pressuring you to buy certain stocks! No one who works in the discount brokerage area of a bank is on commission.

People who use this service must do their own research. There are a variety of sources available to assist in this process. The financial and business press, advisory services and individual investment advisors are examples of such sources.

Discount brokers do:

1. Process buy and sell orders,
2. Hold securities for government-insured safe-keeping,
3. Provide records for tax purposes.

By establishing a brokerage account with a bank, you can buy or sell securities simply by calling the appropriate telephone number. Banks usually enhance this service with another attractive feature. Most offer you the advantage of banking and brokerage accounts combined. If you have a checking or savings account with the bank, it's usually possible to request that purchases be debited and sales proceeds credited to the account you personally select (i.e., NOW, Money Market). Thus, you're no longer obligated to mail in a check or show up in person every time you want to execute an order. Once your orders are executed, banks normally mail you confirmations detailing all transactions.

Customers are usually given the option of taking delivery of their purchases (i.e., stock certificates) or using the bank's safekeeping services. If you authorized the bank to safekeep securities, they retain the actual documents furnishing you with a receipt of what is being held.

What about dividends and interest earned on securities held in safekeeping?

Most banks will automatically credit to a designated account (i.e., checking, savings) any dividends or interest earned on instruments held in safekeeping.

Banks, especially in larger cities, are fairly competitive when it comes to the discount brokerage business. Prices change frequently. Fees vary significantly. Some banks charge extra for record-keeping services while others don't. Cost may be determined by the stock's selling price, the number of shares traded or a mixture of the two. If your transaction constitutes less than a specific amount, a minimum charge may be assessed. Maintenance fees may or may not be charged for safekeeping services.

In short, what makes up the fees is only limited by the creativity of bank management.

Our point is —

SHOP AROUND FOR A DISCOUNT BROKER.

Find out what goes into their fee calculations. Some institutions find it cost advantageous to establish accounts with different institutions. Discount brokers are often classified as "share brokers" or "value brokers". To help you understand why anyone would establish multiple accounts, let's define what we mean by the above classifications.

Share brokers determine charges mainly by the number of shares traded. If you're purchasing only a few shares, such as 50 shares of a $60 stock, these brokers are usually cheaper.

Value brokers weigh their fees by the amount of a transaction. If you're buying numerous shares of a low-priced stock, such as 500 shares of a $4 stock, a value broker will usually make you the best deal.

Of course you can always compromise. Choose a discount broker with a mixed "share/value" price formula.

More and more banks are offering discount brokerage services. But as we said earlier, bankers aren't the only people marketing this service. They do, however, possess a competitive edge when it comes to simplifying transactions — the sale amount can almost always be *automatically* credited or debited to other personal accounts.

Discount brokerage isn't for everyone. If you're seeking investment advice, then pay the price and visit a professional stockbroker. However, if you number among those who prefer to make their own investment decisions, then discount brokerage is certainly an idea worth exploring.

Chapter 6

Government Securities

W hat do banks and government securities have in common? Banks sell government securities. You could say they act as a broker for them. Moneys they collect from purchases *do not* remain with them. With the exception of U. S. Savings Bonds, banks assess fees for handling such transactions. Fee structures are designed to cover associated expenses *and* increase bank profits. Most brokerage houses also sell many of the instruments categorized as "government securities." However, fees assessed by brokerage houses are often higher than those set by banks.

Government securities are popular investment vehicles. Let's take a look at some of the reasons why they appeal to people.

1. They're safe. Regardless of the amount you purchase, the United States government or one of its agencies stands behind them.
2. Buyers are guaranteed the return of principal and interest. Depending on the type of security involved, it may be necessary to hold the instrument until maturity to realize the *full* amount of the principal and interest.
3. Any interest earned is not taxable at the state or local level (only a few exceptions exist in the area of agency instruments).
4. They're very liquid. Depending on the instrument, it's easy to cash it in (i.e., U. S. Savings Bonds) or sell it (i.e., U. S. Treasury Bills).
5. Buyers can choose from a variety of maturities, interest rates, minimum amounts, etc.
6. With the exception of U. S. Savings Bonds, government securities can be traded on the open market

just like corporate stocks. Profits (and we're not talking about interest earnings) can potentially be made by buying and selling these instruments.

The United States government and its agencies sell securities to investors in order to raise money. What's this money used for? It helps pay expenses. In other words, they can't pay all of their bills without borrowing money.

Interest rates are determined by market conditions and demand. If there's a surplus of money, rates go down. If money is tight yet in demand, rates go up. We've just given you a simplified explanation of what "high finance" is all about!

Have you noticed that on more than one occasion we've alluded to the availability of different types of government securities?

Let's take a look at the various instruments commonly referred to as government securities.

U. S. Savings Bonds

The U. S. Savings Bond program underwent quite a face-lift in November 1982. Interest rates escalated, deregulation allowed the banking community to introduce several new instruments attractive to the average investor and many people stopped buying savings bonds. Rates were too low; no consideration was given to market conditions. Only by revamping the program could Washington compete with other borrowers.

You can buy series EE or series HH savings bonds. To help you understand their similarities and differences, we've included separate sections highlighting characteristics of each.

Series EE — The new series EE bonds allow you to earn competitive interest rates without risking principal.

EE bonds can be purchased at most banks, Federal Reserve Banks and Branches, and the Bureau of Public Debt.

Also, many employers participate in a payroll deduction program. By pre-authorizing your employer, money can be withheld from your check and used to purchase bonds in you name. These bonds are then physically delivered to you (they're usually included with your pay check).

The new series EE bonds are designed to keep pace with the market rates. However, your savings are protected from market downswings with a guaranteed minimum return of 7.5%.

Here's how market-based interest works.

On May 1 and November 1 of each year, the Treasury Department sets the market-based rate for the following six-month interest period. This rate is 85% of the average market return during the preceding six months on marketable Treasury securities. If the calculated rate is less than 7.5%, you will still earn 7.5%. Interest is compounded semiannually.

SERIES EE SAVINGS BONDS DENOMINATIONS TABLE	
Issue Price	Face* Amount
$ 25.00	$ 50.00
$ 37.50	$ 75.00
$ 50.00	$ 100.00
$ 100.00	$ 200.00
$ 250.00	$ 500.00
$ 500.00	$ 1,000.00
$2,500.00	$ 5,000.00
$5,000.00	$10,000.00

*Face amount is guaranteed if bond is held for 10 years.

Bonds held less than five years earn interest on a fixed, graduated scale starting at 5.5% after one year and rising by 0.25% every six months thereafter until five years have passed. By holding series EE bonds five years or more, you'll earn interest at the average of 10 or more market-based rates or a minimum of 7.5%. A bond's face value represents its worth after 10 years if the guaranteed minimum rate of 7.5% is applied. However, a bond will reach its face value much faster if the market-based rate remains higher.

Annual purchases of series EE bonds are limited to $30,000 face amount ($15,000 issue price). If two people are listed as co-owners, the limit applies to each. Thus, a maximum of $60,000 face amount ($30,000 issue price) applies if two people purchase bonds as co-owners.

Series EE savings bonds have been sold by the United State government for more than four decades. Many people purchased bonds years ago and have yet to redeem them even though their maturity dates are long past. One word of caution — bonds issued before April 1952 cease to earn interest exactly

40 years after issue date. If you own one of these matured bonds, they should be redeemed or converted to series HH bonds.

Series HH — Series H bonds were introduced in 1952. Note that we specified "H" rather than "HH".

Series H bonds are no longer sold. Series HH bonds are available only on an exchange basis. Eligible Series E (the predecessor of our current EE bonds) and present EE bonds with a redemption value of $500 or more may be converted to Series HH bonds. Proceeds from redeemed series H bonds may also be used to purchase series HH bonds. The latter are issued only by Federal Reserve Banks and Branches and the Bureau of Public Debt. However, most banks and other financial institutions will accept and forward exchange applications along with the bonds being exchanged to the nearest Federal Reserve Bank or Branch. The new bonds will then be delivered by mail in accordance with the purchaser's instructions.

HH bonds issued on or after November 1, 1982, earn 7.5% interest annually. It is paid semiannually; checks issued by the Treasury Department are mailed to bondholders.

SERIES HH BONDS TABLE

Bond Denominations	Semiannual Interest Checks
$ 500.00	$ 18.75
$ 1,000.00	$ 37.50
$ 5,000.00	$187.50
$10,000.00	$375.00

Series HH bonds mature 10 years after purchase date.

Unlike series EE bonds, there are no annual limitations. Any amount of HH bonds may be acquired in any given year.

Now let's summarize some of the features shared by both series.

U.S. Savings Bonds may be registered in any of the following ownerships:

Single ownership — one adult or one minor is named as the owner.

Co-ownership — two people are named as co-owners. Either person may cash the bond.

Beneficiary — one owner and one beneficiary is named. During the owner's lifetime, only the owner may cash the bond.

Bonds cannot be transferred, sold or used as collateral.

Can bonds be redeemed at anytime?

Yes, with a few exceptions. A bond cannot be redeemed during the first six months following its purchase date. HH bonds have an additional stipulation. If an HH bond is received for redemption purposes during the month preceding an interest payment date, it will not be redeemed until that date. Most banks and other financial institutions will redeem series EE bonds without charge. Series HH bonds must be forwarded to a Federal Reserve Bank or Branch or the Bureau of Public Debt. Most banks, however, will assist in this process at no cost to you.

Like other government securities, U.S. Savings Bonds offer the investor tax advantages. Interest is not taxed on the state or local level. In the case of series EE bonds, federal taxes on the interest may be deferred until you cash in the bond. Money you don't lose through annual taxation earns additional interest. Thus, your bond's effective yield goes up!

Many people defer interest until retirement, so as to reduce the tax bite. Since retirement generally brings with it a lower tax bracket (don't forget if you're over 65, you also get a double exemption), once the bonds are redeemed less interest is lost through taxes.

Interest earned on series HH bonds, however, *cannot* be deferred. Such interest is subject to federal tax each year it is paid.

All U.S. Savings Bonds are subject to other taxes regardless of whether they are federal or state. Examples are estate, inheritance and gift taxes.

If your bonds are lost, stolen or destroyed, the Treasury Department will replace them free. Simply notify the Bureau of

Public Debt, 200 Third Street, Parkersburg, WV 26101. If possible, include serial numbers (with prefix and suffix letters), issue dates (month and year), SSN's or EIN's, names and addresses applicable to the missing bonds. Our best advice, if you buy bonds, is to record the above information and keep it in a safe place separate from the bonds.

Treasury Bills

Treasury bills are often referred to as "T-bills."

A Treasury bill is an obligation of the United States government to pay the bearer a fixed sum after a specified number of days from the date of issue. It is an interest-bearing security, and it matures in one year or less.

The U.S. Treasury bill is probably the best known, most popular short-term investment medium issued by the government. T-bills are presently issued in four maturities — 91 days, 6 months, 9 months and 1 year.

These instruments are sold at a discount through competitive bidding at weekly auctions held by the Treasury Department. These auctions are held every Monday. If Monday is a holiday, the auction takes place on the preceding Friday. Although interest rates are actually established on auction day, bank personnel responsible for handling these transactions can usually give you a fairly good idea ahead of time what to expect in interest rates.

The investor's return is the difference between the purchase price and the face or par value. The rate of return on a Treasury bill of a given maturity is calculated by dividing the discount by par and expressing this percentage as an annual rate, using a 360-day year. For example, a price of $97.640 per $100 of face amount for a 91-day bill would produce an annual rate of return equal to 9.336%.

$$\frac{100 - 97.640}{100} \times \frac{360}{91} = 9.336\%$$

As indicated above, T-bills are sold in "discount" form. When you buy a new issue, you pay the full face value (i.e., $10,000 for a $10,000 bill). The Federal Reserve will immediately send you a smaller check, prepaying the interest your security will earn over its life.

A T-bill is redeemable for full face value on its maturity date.

What if you need the money prior to maturity?

T-bills can be sold prior to maturity. Most larger banks as well as brokerage houses will handle such transactions for a fee. You will receive less than face value — the difference represents the interest on the T-bill which the buyer is to receive. By the same process, if you wish to purchase a T-bill that matures in a specific week, you can buy an old one rather than a new issue.

Interest paid on T-bills is taxable for the year it's received. Realize, however, that such interest is only taxable on a federal level. T-bill interest is free from state or local taxation.

Treasury Notes

People often refer to Treasury notes as T-notes.

T-notes come in multiples of $1,000. They mature between one and ten years. Interest is payable semiannually.

The Treasury Department sells these instruments through auctions. Unlike T-bills, sales of new issues are not held on a weekly basis. Two-year notes are auctioned once a month. Longer-term notes of varying maturities are auctioned quarterly.

Until a few years ago, T-notes were generally sold in "bearer" form. This means that the actual certificate has no name on it. In order to collect semiannual interest payments, you had to clip coupons and then redeem them at a Federal Reserve Bank or Branch or your local bank. These coupons were printed along the sides and bottom of the note.

Since January 1983, however, all U.S. Treasury notes have been issued in "registered" form. In other words, the certificate is actually registered in someone's name. The note itself has the owner's name and SSN printed on it; checks for semiannual interest payments are automatically sent to owners.

A T-note is redeemable for full face value on its maturity date. If you wish to receive money for one of these instruments prior to maturity date, it can be sold. For a fee, most larger banks as well as brokerage houses will handle such transactions. Whether you receive full face value depends on market conditions. A T-note can be a long-term investment. Its current market value depends largely on the interest rate it is earning. Depending on rates associated with new issues, the market value of old issues can fluctuate. For example, if new issues earn 7% interest and you wish to purchase an older issue earning 13% interest, you would probably have to pay premium for it (in this case, by "premium" we mean more than face value). Thus, your effective yield won't really be 13%.

Interest paid on T-notes is taxable for the year it's received. Interest is taxable only on a federal level; it remains free from state and local taxes.

Treasury Bonds

U.S. Treasury bonds, or rather T-bonds, are obligations issued by the federal government. Maturities range from 5 years to several decades. They are sold in multiples of $1,000.

The market value associated with a T-bond, however, can be greater or less than its face value. Market value depends basically on whether current interest rates are lower or higher than the rates on the day the bond was issued. If you wish to receive money for a T-bond prior to its maturity, how much you receive will depend on current market conditions. By the same rule, if you purchase an old issue rather than a new one, how much you'll have to pay depends on existing market conditions.

Some longer term issues are callable. This means that the Treasury Department has the option to retire them at face value several years prior to maturity. If the government exercises this option, all bondholders of the issue being retired will receive full face value at the time these instruments are called.

How do you know if a T-bond is callable?

If an issue is callable, the final year of maturity as well as the first year in which the call privilege may be exercised is cited on the security itself.

Old issue T-bonds which sell for less than face value may be attractive for a couple of reasons.

First, the government rarely exercises its option to redeem such bonds at the earliest possible date. Why would the government be willing to pay $1,000 for a bond that is only selling for $900 on the open market?

Second, there are potential tax advantages to be reaped by the investor who purchases bonds selling below face value. Long-term bonds typically increase in market value as their maturity dates approach. These increases in market value are taxable as capital gains. For example, if you purchased a $1,000 T-bond for $990, that $10 difference is taxed as a capital gain. Realize this $10 profit has absolutely nothing to do with interest. The bond will continue to earn whatever interest rate is associated with the issue regardless of how much it's discounted. Capital gains may be taxable at federal, state and local levels. But if you buy a discounted bond and own it for at least a year before selling it, then you will be taxed at a substantially lower capital gains rate (at least on the federal level). The key is not to sell the instrument for at least *one year*.

Interest earned on Treasury bonds is taxable only on a federal level. It is free from state or local taxation.

The interest paid on one of these instruments is often called the "coupon" rate. This name is derived from the fact that coupons must be clipped from bonds to collect interest. Interest is paid semiannually.

There is indeed an active market for T-bonds. Buyers for old issues are easy to find. Handling such transactions, however, does require the assistance of a bank or brokerage house. Fees are charged for such services, thus reducing your effective annual yield.

Government Agency Bonds

The U.S. Treasury Department isn't the only branch of our government that borrows money. More than 100 different bond issues are sold by various government agencies. Like Treasury securities, bonds can be purchased by individuals with the assistance of a bank or brokerage house.

Some of the better known bond issuers falling in this category are Federal Home Loan Bank, Federal Land Bank, Federal Intermediate Credit Bank, Federal Housing Administration, Federal Intermediate Credit Bank and Bank for Cooperatives. Agency bonds usually pay 1% more than T-bonds. Maturities and denominations vary depending on the issuing agency.

If you invest in these securities, be aware there are relatively few buyers and sellers. If you hold the bond to maturity, a limited market is no problem. But if you plan to sell one early, realize that since there are few traders you may not get the most desirable price.

Interest on agency securities are subject to federal income taxes, but again — with a few exceptions — are not subject to state or local taxes.

With the exception of U.S. Savings Bonds, banks transact, sell, and purchase orders for government securities for a fee. Fees vary. They typically range from $35 to $60. Let's say your local bank charges $50 to assist in the purchase of a 2-year T-note earning 12.7% interest. If you account for this $50 fee, your yield is reduced to 12.45%.

If you plan to invest in Treasury or Agency securities, we recommend that you shop around for the best deal. Fees can be determined by more than just executing your orders. Whether you wish to take delivery of instruments or authorize the bank to place them in safekeeping can influence charges. If the bank places one of these instruments in safekeeping, it will be responsible for clipping any coupons and redeeming the instrument upon maturity. Moneys resulting from such acts may be automatically credited to your personal account or perhaps mailed to you in the form of a check.

For the average investor, government securities no longer hold the same attraction they once held. There was a day when investing in these instruments was the only way to secure interest rates better than those offered with passbook savings accounts. Deregulation has changed the market. Rates competitive with government securities can now be had with Money Market checking accounts and CDs.

So why do people and other entities such as corporations still buy government securities?

There are definite tax advantages. As we've repeatedly emphasized, interest earned on almost all of the instruments falling in this category are tax free on state and local levels. Also, if you choose to liquidate them prior to maturity you will not be assessed penalties. You do, however, risk a downswing in the market; thus, you may not recover full face value.

Chapter 7

Trust Services

T rust Departments aren't just for the rich! Today's multi-dimensional Trust Department caters to a variety of customer needs. If you own a business, travel frequently, have no immediate family in the area, need to make a will, have difficulty keeping track of financial matters, own rental property, desire investment assistance, or are a professional then *you* may be a candidate for this often ignored and misunderstood aspect of the banking business.

We certainly don't intend to give you an in-depth explanation of what Trust Departments do. That alone could fill an entire book! Our purpose in including this section is mainly to introduce those Trust Department services which may benefit the average investor.

But first we want to emphasize two very important facts.

1. Not every bank has a Trust Department.
2. Services rendered and fees charged vary depending on bank policy, size, competition, etc.

Trust services usually represent fee income to bank management. Fees are calculated a variety of ways. A set amount for a particular service, such as will preparation and safekeeping, may be assessed, or a percentage of the moneys involved, such as rental for investment property. Our best advice is ask prior to making any final agreement with the bank.

Trusts

Trust accounts are how the entire concept of Trust Departments evolved. For centuries trusts have helped successful people manage their assets.

Unfortunately, several misconceptions surround these accounts.

1. Only the very wealthy can benefit from them —WRONG!
2. Once established, they cannot be amended. — WRONG!
3. There are no lifetime advantages to people who establish them. — WRONG!

A trust can help you manage your assets — during your lifetime and after your death. Trust administrators are professionals trained in such areas as investments, taxes, and law. Does this administrator have a totally free hand when it comes to making investment decisions? It depends on how you establish the trust. These accounts can be as flexible or as rigid as you want.

There are different types of trust accounts.

A *living trust* is sometimes referred to as an investment agency account. It is established during a person's lifetime and can continue after death for the heir and/or designated beneficiaries. Living trusts are further defined as:

1. *Revocable* — The trust may be amended or cancelled at any time as family or financial circumstances change.
2. *Irrevocable* — The trust cannot be amended.

A living trust can prove especially helpful when people become unavailable to manage their affairs due to extended travel, illness or disability at a time when crucial decisions may be needed. Along with professional asset management, record keeping services are provided. Income tax advantages may be reaped. An estate is better protected against death taxes. Estate settlement remains confidential, since a trust can eliminate the publicity of probate. Charitable gifts can be made while still retaining lifetime benefits from assets involved. Inheritances are better protected from losses due to poor asset management by heirs.

If you create a *testamentary trust*, it will not become effective until after your death. Conditions associated with such a trust must be contained in a person's will.

A testamentary trust provides an equitable distribution of an estate. It also provides professional asset management for heirs and/or beneficiaries until such distribution is made.

Although testamentary and living trusts afford many of the same advantages, important differences can exist. If the validity or terms of the will creating the testamentary trust are successfully challenged in court, the terms of the trust might also be invalidated. Testamentary trusts do not afford certain income tax and estate tax breaks. Nor do they create safeguards to provide management for property when the will's administrator is unavailable due to illness, travel, etc. Also, probate is not avoided by establishing a testamentary trust.

One of the major advantages realized with this type of trust is professional asset management and record keeping for heirs and/or beneficiaries. Since heirs are often inexperienced and/or unqualified to manage an estate, inheritances are better protected. Also, circumstances which require special planning can be handled such as minor children and handicapped or elderly family members.

Executorships

Trust Departments are often named as *executors* of wills. An executor is named in a will by the person making it. This individual or corporation, in the case of a bank, carries out the provisions stated in the will and assumes responsibility for winding up the deceased person's personal and business affairs.

Examples of tasks handled by an executor are:

1. An assessment and inventory of all estate assets is made.
2. Any moneys owed to the estate are collected.
3. Debts and all taxes (i.e., income, estate, inheritance) are paid. Moneys for such payments are taken from the estate.
4. Business and financial decisions required for the settlement of an estate are made (i.e., how cash should be invested, which securities should be sold).
5. Estate assets are distributed.
6. Accountings related to the settlement of an estate are made to the proper authorities (i.e., Federal Estate Tax Return, State Tax reports related to inheritances).

If mistakes are made in the performance of any duties associated with an executorship, the executor is responsible for reimbursing the estate for any resulting loss.

Naming a bank as executor of a will offers several distinct advantages. Family members are relieved of duties which can require detailed legal, financial, and accounting knowledge. Continual professional asset management is assured during the administration of an estate. By naming a corporate executor, you avoid placing a friend or relative in an awkward position if disagreements arise among heirs which require the executor to make decisions. Using Trust Department personnel guarantees the presence of a full-time experienced executor who will not become unavailable due to illness, travel or other responsibilities. Since Trust Department personnel are very familiar with taxes associated with estate settlement, they are more likely to reduce an estate's tax expense by filing returns on time and using all allowable deductions.

Before wrapping up our discussion on executorships, we have one last, very interesting note to add. If an individual is named as an executor rather than a Trust Department, many banks offer estate settlement assistance to this individual. The latter is usually a fee-based service.

Investment Agencies

You don't have to establish a trust to enlist the investment expertise offered by Trust Departments. They will help you invest moneys by providing continual advice or full management for individual and corporate investment portfolios. When serving in such capacities, Trust Departments are functioning as "agents."

There are three basic types of investment accounts available.

1. *Investment Advisory Account* — Customer approval is required before securities are purchased or sold.
2. *Investment Management Account* — Recognizing the risk tolerance and account objectives established by the customer, Trust Departments can make independent investment decisions. This investment agreement is always subject to amendment or termination by customer request.
3. *Custodial Account* — No investment services are rendered; only custodial services are involved.

Two of the above account types involve investment decisions. They, too, include custodial services. Let's detail what custodial services provide.

Assets are safekept, income and proceeds from securities are collected, securities are purchased and sold at customers' requests, and funds are disbursed in accordance with customers' requests. Custodial services also insure that the customer will be notified about such asset related matters as stock splits and bond calls. Customers receive statements detailing all transactions along with annual tax statements.

Investment accounts are popular for several reasons. Along with affording custodial services, they offer objective investment advice from trained professionals. A more diversified portfolio is usually developed. And it's easy to convert an investment account to a trust account.

Escrow

Trust Departments can act as escrow agents. Now let's define what escrows are all about.

Business transactions involving money, securities, or other types of property must sometimes be temporarily deposited with a disinterested third party. These funds are retained by the escrow agent until all terms of the escrow agreement have been satisfactorily met. At this time, the escrow agent delivers all property held in the account to those parties specified in the agreement. Delivery terms such as the amounts involved are specified in the escrow agreement.

People and/or companies who have adverse interests yet share business dealings often establish escrows. Escrows insure that the terms of their business agreements will be carried out under the scrutiny of a disinterested third party with recognized creditability. Real estate ventures are popular candidates for this particular bank service.

Real Estate Management

Most Trust Departments offer real estate management services. Residential and/or commercial property is sometimes placed in Trust accounts. Investment accounts may also include real estate holdings. But regardless of whether you have other financial relationships with a Trust Department, you may elect to have a bank assist in the management or development of residential or commercial property.

Real estate services rendered by bank Trust Departments may include:

1. Advertise and show property to prospective tenants or buyers.
2. Screen and select tenants by taking applications, conducting personal interviews, and obtaining credit reports on prospective tenants.
3. Draft and negotiate leases.
4. Collect rent and monitor delinquencies.
5. Handle tenant complaints.
6. Pay bills and expenses out of moneys collected or out of other funds designated by owner(s) for such purposes.
7. Review insurance coverage and pay premiums when due.
8. Arrange for necessary repairs or improvements which may increase investment return.
9. Act as a broker in the buying or selling of property.
10. Prepare and file applicable tax returns.
11. Distribute profits to owner(s). This distribution may be in the form of checks or deposits to designated accounts.

If you use the real estate management services offered by most Trust Departments, you should receive an annual statement which will assist in the preparation of your personal tax returns. A detailed record of all income and expenses is usually included (i.e., rentals, capital gains, depreciation).

If you invest in real estate, authorizing a bank to manage your property has several advantages. Someone is always available to handle tenant complaints, repairs, etc. Tax information is prepared by professionals. If multiple owners are involved, a bank affords centralized management. And they can offer objective advice regarding the buying, selling, or improving of property.

Timber and Mineral Management

When property is involved, one person may own the land while another owns the timber or mineral rights. Property is sometimes sold while these rights are placed in trusts for heirs. Such rights may also be part of an investment account. And like real estate management, regardless of whether other account relationships exist, individuals or corporations can authorize most Trust Departments to manage their timber and mineral rights.

These management services include drafting, negotiating and reviewing leases. Royalties will be collected and the resulting income disbursed. Investment returns may be reviewed periodically to determine whether they justify continued retention of the rights.

Detailed records are usually sent to all owners on at least an annual basis. Such records can assist in the preparation of tax returns. These records generally include depletion allowances, capital gains, expenses, and income.

Timber and mineral rights often include several people, especially when they are inherited. In such cases, a Trust Department provides centralized management. They streamline the distribution of income and furnish all owners with tax-related information.

Retirement Plans

If you're self-employed, a professional, or the owner of a business, Trust Departments can help you plan a better retirement. Most offer a broad spectrum of retirement products. Their plans include pensions, defined contributions, profit sharing, thrift savings, stock bonus, deferred compensation, Keoghs for the self-employed, and IRAs. A combination of plans may even be prescribed.

Trust Department personnel keep abreast of the many complex legal regulations affecting retirement plans. They know what the current IRS rulings are and how they impact your particular plan. Other benefits reaped from bank-managed plans include assistance in tax reporting requirements. If you own a business, Trust personnel may be available to meet with your employees to discuss plan benefits. The bank will annually allocate assets to plan participants and prepare supporting statements for the employer.

Financial Planning

One of the newest and most progressive products marketed by an increasing number of Trust Departments is Financial Planning.

We live in a constantly changing financial environment. Comprehensive planning for both the present and future is necessary to ensure sound finances for you and your family. Your plan must be flexible enough to accommodate changes in laws, the economy and family circumstances.

Financial planning is often divided into two categories.

Current planning provides net worth and cash flor analysis. Income tax and retirement strategies are mapped out. It concentrates on the state of your financial affairs during your lifetime.

Estate planning concentrates on how your estate will be handled after death. Objectives must be established. Determining whether your assets can meet these objectives is an important part of this process. How your estate will be distributed among your heirs is discussed. Trust personnel help you provide liquidity to pay any debts and taxes. Furthermore, they help you design inheritances which can minimize income and death taxes.

What's Direct Deposit?

D irect deposit" is a banking service which allows moneys to be credited or debited to designated accounts without using such traditional paper documents as checks or invoices.

Direct deposit as we know it could not exist without the aid of computers. It is entirely a product of the hi-tech age we live in. In fact, one of the first names attached to this particular service was Electronic Funds Transfer or EFT for short. Today, the technical name for this service is ACH processing.

ACH stands for Automated Clearing House. The first automated clearing house was established in 1972. It was created for the express purpose of allowing financial institutions, government agencies, and companies to exchange paperless entries. Located in California, it was referred to as CACHA (California Automated Clearing House Association).

In 1974 the National Automated Clearing House Association (NACHA) was formed to develop and coordinate a nationwide ACH network. Initially, each ACH operated on a local basis only. Joint efforts between NACHA and the Federal Reserve System, however, resulted in late 1977 in a project which changed the business of direct deposit forever. They successfully developed and introduced procedures which would allow financial transactions to be quickly routed through local ACHs to their end destination. The result was a nationwide ACH network. Today a direct deposit item can be originated by a company in Maine and credited to someone's account in California within days.

Five entities participate in our present system. They are:

1. *Customer* — The customer is the person who authorizes direct deposit activity.

2. *Company* — The company is the entity that generates the direct deposit transactions.

3. *Originating Depository Financial Institution* — The originating depository financial institution (ODFI) is the institution that receives direct deposit transactions from participating companies. These transactions are then forwarded to a central clearing facility.

4. *Automated Clearing House* — An automated clearing house (ACH) is the central clearing facility that receives direct deposit transactions from ODFIs. The ACH in turn sends these transactions to the appropriate financial institutions.

5. *Receiving Depository Financial Institution* — The receiving depository financial institution (RDFI) is the institution that receives direct deposit transactions from an ACH. These transactions are then posted to customers' accounts.

Now that we've defined the players in the game, let's put them to work in a typical direct deposit situation.

Thousands of people have their social security payments automatically deposited to a checking or savings account each month. If you're one of these people, then you are the customer. The Social Security Administration is the company. Using computers, this government agency creates electronic entries which will eventually be used by your bank to credit your account. The Social Security Administration's ODFI routes thousands of electronically generated SS payments to the regional ACH. This ACH then distributes these transactions throughout the United States. The local ACH used by your bank finally receives the transaction. It then forwards this transaction to your bank where it is credited to the account you have specified.

Although it may sound time consuming, this entire process occurs within days. If you are one of the thousands who already have their social security payments deposited directly to a bank account, then you know it is always accomplished on time. In fact, direct deposit can even beat the mail!

Social Security payments are but the tip of the iceberg when it comes to exploring the world of direct deposit. An increasing number of companies are offering their employees the opportunity to have their pay amounts automatically deposited to designated bank accounts. Insurance companies are automatically crediting physicians' accounts with payments. Banks even use ACHs to transfer funds between financial institutions. For example, you might open up a Christmas Club account at Main Street Bank but wish to make payments from a checking account located at East Boulevard Bank. Of course you could write checks, but an automatic deposit would be more convenient. If your bank wishes to do so, ACH processing can accommodate this.

Realize, though, that more than likely your bank will not agree to every direct deposit request you make. It's not because they don't want to, but that the supporting computer links may not be available. For example, your bank's computers may not be programmed to handle direct deposits for Christmas Club accounts.

Direct deposit isn't the only banking function handled via ACH processing. Just as you can credit accounts, so can you debit accounts. The latter is sometimes referred to as "preauthorized bill payments."

Companies with billing operations may utilize our nationwide ACH network by creating electronic transactions for bill payments. You, as a customer, may grant a participating company authority to initiate periodic charges to a designated account as bills become due. Situations in which recurring bills are regular and do not vary in amount are ideal candidates for this service. You can easily plan ahead of time to have sufficient funds deposited to cover these charges. Popular examples of preauthorized bill payments are insurance premiums and mortgage payments.

To use the bill payment feature, does the amount have to be constant?

No. For example, some utility companies use ACH processing to charge customers' accounts. If amounts do vary, be sure adequate account balances are maintained.

Can a company just "out of the blue" charge or credit your account with an ACH transaction?

No. If someone wanted to credit your account for $500, we doubt if many would protest. However, just imagine how angry you'd be if $500 mysteriously disappeared from one of your bank accounts!

Neither direct deposits nor preauthorized bill payments can be made without customer authorization. Look closely at the descriptive term "preauthorized bill payment." The word "preauthorized" clues you in to the fact that some type of authorization is required before any real activity can occur.

First, you must sign a form with any company (i.e., corporation, bank, government agency) that intends to access one of your accounts via the ACH network. If you wish to allow different types of transactions, corresponding authorizations must be given regardless of whether the same company is involved. In other words, if you want your insurance company to automatically charge your checking account for both life and home insurance premiums, separate authorizations must be granted.

Once the authorization form is signed, the company usually generates an electronic transaction called a "prenotification." These transactions are generated for zero dollar amounts. A prenotification entry should be created at least 10 days prior to the first live transaction. This process helps ensure that the designated account number actually exists for the customer and that the account is active rather than dormant. Prenotification is not required by law. However, most companies subscribe to this practice, especially if bill payment is involved.

What we've attempted to do up until now is to present you with a general overview of what ACH is all about. Hopefully we've acquainted you with several new terms as well as defined others you may have previously encountered, but never fully understood, such as "direct deposit."

For the remainder of this chapter, we want to focus on how you as a consumer can benefit from this hi-tech banking service.

Automated deposits offer the average consumer several advantages. One of the most noticeable benefits is the consistent availability of funds on a timely basis, even during vacation, illness, or business trips. Direct deposit eliminates the possibility of lost or stolen checks. How many times have you heard tragic stories about someone's Social Security checks being stolen? Unfortunately, there are those with less than desirable motives who canvass neighborhoods heavily populated with senior citizens for the sole purpose of stealing their Social Security checks. Direct deposit also eliminates you having to take the time to manually deposit checks.

Preauthorized bill payment also has its advantages. No longer do you have to write as many checks. Postage expenses as well as the cost of checks are eliminated. Service charges associated with both checking and savings accounts can vary depending on whether a transaction is ACH or check generated. ACH transactions are almost always cheaper when it comes to calculating service fees. Many banks even develop service fee structures which allow any number of ACH transactions to be posted without incurring any service charges. They do this to encourage electronic transactions. The latter are cheaper for banks to process because they are paperless. Any time a paper transaction is encountered, considerable overhead goes with it (i.e., proof encoding, microfilming, statement stuffing).

Another noteworthy benefit is the avoidance of late payments. Paying bills late often results in extra interest charges or penalties. By ensuring timely payments will always be made, you establish an excellent payment and credit record.

Since ACH transactions are paperless entries to your account, how do you know what has transpired?

ACH transactions are considered paperless, because you are not furnished with a piece of paper describing the transaction each time one occurs. For example, if you go to a teller window and deposit a check, the teller will give you a receipt. On the other hand, if the Social Security Administration deposits your monthly Social Security payment in your checking account, no teller will be giving you a receipt.

The bank will, however, furnish you with a descriptive statement. Federal regulations dictate that customers whose accounts experience ACH activity be furnished with periodic statements descriptively detailing such transactions. Information which must be disclosed includes the posting date, dollar amount, name of company originating the transaction, a description of the transaction, indication of the type of account involved (i.e., checking, savings), and the account number receiving the electronic debit or credit. Furthermore, the bank must indicate the amount of any charges assessed for ACH activity. Although in actuality banks rarely charge for the handling of such transactions, they can legally assess fees for posting ACH transactions. Since electronically generated entries are considerably cheaper to process than traditional paper documents, banks rarely charge any associated processing fees. Balances as of the beginning and close of the current statement period must be specified. To assist in customer inquiries or error reporting, banks must supply customers with an address and telephone number designated for such notification purposes. An example of a direct deposit transaction descriptively disclosed:

6-8-85 $649.55   Blue Ridge Bank, N.A.
                          Salary

How often descriptive statements must be issued is regulated by law. Applicable regulations basically state that if preauthorized bill payments are made, monthly statements must be rendered; if direct deposits are made, quarterly statements must be issued.

Capitalizing on the existence of our nationwide ACH network to debit and credit people's accounts is an idea still gaining momentum with banks, government agencies, and private businesses. New uses are constantly being discovered. More companies than ever are offering their employees the option of having earnings automatically deposited to personal bank accounts. For you, the average consumer, all of this means greater convenience. No longer do you have to write checks or actually visit a bank or branch to handle many routine aspects of your personal finances, however complex they may be.

Chapter 9

Automatic Transfer Services

M any routine banking chores no longer require a trip to your bank or branch. "Convenience" is the keyword for the 80s. ATMs are springing up everywhere from bowling alleys to airport terminals. Our nationwide ACH network enables millions of people to have their paychecks automatically deposited to a selected bank account. The idea of using computer terminals to support an idea called "home banking" is already making inroads in some parts of the United States. But nowhere is the "convenience factor" more apparent than when automatic transfers of funds are involved.

Marketed by countless banks nationwide, automatic transfer plans are excellent examples of how automation can benefit both bankers and consumers. Although such transfers can be handled manually by bank personnel using tickler files, most larger institutions opt for computer support.

Before proceeding to explain the "ins-and-outs" of the automatic transfer business, let's briefly discuss how computers have improved this particular banking service.

1. Computers don't forget. Payments or deposits made via such plans always occur on time.
2. Computers won't make such common errors as transposing figures (i.e., $212.00 rather than $221.00).
3. High volume processing can be quickly accomplished. Because computers will process hundreds of such transfers within minutes, banks tend to offer their customers a wider variety of services (i.e., savings to checking, CD interest to MMICs,

Installment Loan payments from checking). On the other hand, if manual tickler systems are used, it's doubtful most institutions would be eager to increase their product line since, more than likely, additional staff would be required.

4. Computer-generated transfers are cheaper when it comes to operating overhead.

Now, let's define what we mean by "automatic transfer plans."

An automatic transfer plan allows for the automatic transfer of funds between designated bank accounts. Money is deducted from one account and credited to another without any customer involvement. Banking actively continues regardless of vacations, illness, other obligations, etc.

Are you confused by now as to the difference between ACH processing and automatic transfers?

In simple terms, the former involves money being transferred between different companies or financial institutions while the latter involves only one institution. In other words, one is external and the other one internal.

What if the balance of the account being charged isn't sufficient to cover the amount being deducted?

Naturally, the transfer won't be successful. Customer contact will be required. If a loan payment is involved, late charges may be incurred.

It is the customer's responsibility to maintain adequate account balances. If you participate in automatic transfer plans, you know the *when* and *how much* (in most cases) characteristics of each transfer. Checking accounts, frequently the source of such funds, often come with checkbooks which remind you to mark down all automatic charges. Along with keeping adequate funds available, remember not to use the same money twice! In other words, if you have a $100 IRA contribution due, mark it down in your checkbook so you won't use the $100 for something else.

Some of the more popular bank products frequently utilizing this service are Christmas Clubs, Installment Loans, Mortgage Loans, IRAs, regular savings, and CDs. But *how* the automatic transfer feature relates to a product depends on the product itself. In some cases, payments are being made (i.e., Christmas Clubs) whereas in others interest is being credited (i.e., CDs). Along with being convenient, interest credited under such plans becomes available "quicker." You don't have to wait for a check in the mail and then make a trip to the bank to cash it. It's available the same day it's earned.

Overdraft protection is another way consumers often benefit from automatic transfer services. For example, some banks market a plan whereby if funds aren't available in a checking account to cover all items due to be paid, then a designated savings account will be charged. In such instances, the amounts being transferred can obviously vary. Of course this variability does make it more difficult for you to keep informed of exact account balances. Whether that's a problem is a question only you can resolve. It depends on what type of balances you keep, anticipated transactional activity, how the bank informs you of charges, etc.

How do banks inform customers of automatic transfers which occur?

Some banks generate a paper notice indicating the date, amount, account numbers affected, and a description of what has occurred. Customers may be mailed such forms when transactions actually take place or when they receive their statements.

Descriptive statements may be issued in lieu of individual documents. A descriptive statement describes a transaction in more individualized language than such general terms as "DEPOSIT" or "WITHDRAWAL." For example, if an Installment Loan payment is automatically deducted from a checking account, rather than saying just "WITHDRAWAL" a descriptive statement might say "AUTO PAYMENT FOR LOAN 200-634111." (It's also cheaper for a bank to issue descriptive statements rather than paper documents! Think about it. No extra paper, mailing or stuffing expenses!).

How your bank uses the idea of automatic transfer services is limited only by your banker's creativity. Most bankers actively support these plans for a number of reasons.

1. Automatic transfers can be cheaper than manually handling customer-generated transactions, especially when computers and descriptive statements are involved.
2. Payments and deposits occur on time. Money doesn't get "sidetracked."
3. Cross-selling becomes easier. Before automatic payments, interest credits, overdraft coverage, etc. can occur, the customer must establish such accounts.

In fact, some banks like automatic transfers so much they'll even offer you a bonus for participating. Authorize some banks to automatically deduct your loan payments from a checking or savings account, and they'll *lower* the monthly payment. Authorize Christmas Club payments at some banks, and earn a higher interest rate.

If you're interested in eliminating some of those routine banking chores, explore what your bank has to offer in the way of automatic transfers. Already used by millions nationwide, it's an idea growing in popularity as well as applications. Not only can they make banking more convenient, but participating in such plans may also be your ticket to better interest or reduced loan rates — and that can put extra money in *your* pocket.

Chapter 10

Securing Your Investments

I nvestments are assets. When you put your money to work in a bank, you are in fact investing it. In other words, any deposit account should be regarded as an asset.

Throughout this book, we've discussed numerous deposit instruments marketed by banks nationwide. Examples are MMICs, IRAs, Certificates of Deposit, and Treasury Bills. Like any other asset, these deposit instruments should be protected. You wouldn't buy a home and leave it uninsured, would you? Probably not. Buying homeowner's insurance would be a more likely decision, with the policy papers being placed in a safe location.

Bank deposits, too, reap the benefits of insurance. *Chapter 16 — Insurance — How Important Is It?* discusses federal insurance for certain bank deposits. But like your homeowner's policy, there are two aspects to the asset security game.

1. Physical Security
2. Insurance for Financial Stability

Concern #1, physical security, is what we plan on discussing in the next few pages. Why devote separate chapters to the above topics? One reason we separated them is because not every investment made through a bank is subject to insurance. For example, discount brokerage services allow you to purchase stock certificates. However, such certificates are not covered by any type of bank insurance program. They are negotiable assets payable to bearer.

A CD, on the other hand, is subject to federal insurance providing your bank is insured by the FDIC. However, you still have the physical security situation. True, if you look at the actual CD document, you'll probably see the words, "NOT NEGOTIABLE." This means that possession of the physical certificate doesn't mean entitlement to proceeds. These CDs are *not* payable to bearer.

If they are not negotiable, then why does a bank bother to issue such forms?

The certificate spells out what type of agreement has been made between you and the bank. It states what interest rate will be paid. How much the obligation is for is included. (We used the term "obligation" to remind you that when you make a deposit you are, in fact, lending money to a bank. Thus, it becomes their obligation to repay such monies.) Your name, as the purchaser, is typed on this document, along with an authorized bank official's signature.

Why is there a place for an authorized signature by a bank official? Because this agreement we call a Certificate of Deposit is nothing more than a contract between you and the bank. Because it is one form of a contract, this document should be treated with the same care as other important papers.

True, you can still get your money without the physical certificate. Affording you accessibility to funds is the #1 purpose behind signature cards. (We'll talk more about signature cards and authorized signatures in *Chapter 11 — Account Ownership.*) It's a whole lot easier, though, to cash in a CD if you also possess the document itself!

Protecting your valuables and important papers from fire, theft, and loss can be accomplished different ways. Some people buy combination safes. Safes, however, are still physically located in homes. Don't kid yourself! Many a burglar doubles as an expert safecracker. Of course, there's always good old Aunt Faye's method of tucking the goodies underneath mattresses. Common sense, though, dictates that isn't too secure of an approach. Mattresses can burn or be pillaged quite easily.

A better and more sensible approach to securing your investments is to explore two solutions offered by most larger banks:

1. Safe Deposit Boxes
2. Safekeeping Services

Safe Deposit Boxes

When you rent a safe deposit box, what you're really doing is renting space in some bank's vault.

A vault is a necessity for any bank, regardless of size. Vaults are used to house coins and dollar bills, securities customers put up as collateral for loans (i.e., stock certificates), blank U.S. Savings Bonds which will later be sold to customers, Treasury Securities purchased for Trust Accounts, etc. The list is practically endless, since most banks (especially large ones) handle numerous important and often negotiable documents. In fact, some banks have more than one vault.

Along with using vaults to secure personal property directly related to bank business, many banks rent to individuals such as yourself physical space in these secured areas. So, in other words, a *safe deposit box* is simply an area of physical vault space. To isolate each person's secured area and maintain privacy, metal boxes are assigned to each person who rents space. These boxes are placed in slots specially built inside a vault just for this purpose. Each slot is covered with a small door requiring *two* keys to open it. More about these keys later, first let's discuss box size.

Banks usually rent safe deposit boxes on an annual basis, requiring payment in advance. How much this payment is depends on box size. Different sizes are generally available, with rentals scaled accordingly. Jewelry, contracts, birth and marriage certificates, real estate deeds, promissory notes, mortgages, wills, stock and bond certificates are examples of valuable documents commonly kept in safe deposit boxes. What size box you need depends on what you plan to keep in it. Most people need only a small box, since several dozen papers can be folded and stored in even the smallest one.

The following chart illustrates sample box sizes and rates.

SAMPLE BOX SIZES AND RATES	
Size of Box (inches)	**Annual Rent**
2 × 5 × 22	$ 10.00
3 × 5 × 22	$ 13.00
4 × 5 × 22	$ 20.00
3 × 10 × 22	$ 25.00
5 × 10 × 22	$ 32.00
10 × 10 × 22	$ 55.00
10 × 11 × 22	$ 65.00
12 × 10 × 22	$ 80.00
13 × 23 × 22	$160.00

What do the above dimensions represent?

$2 \times 5 \times 22$ translates into:

    2 = depth
    5 = width
    22 = length

A $2 \times 5 \times 22$ inch box is 2 inches deep, 5 inches wide, and 22 inches long.

Banks almost always will require the total cost of a safe deposit box at rental time. Each year thereafter, you will again be asked to pay in advance. A 1-year contract is standard procedure.

This contract spells out certain conditions of the rental arrangement. The fact that payment will be made in advance is one example of these contract terms. Another example is what will occur if keys are lost. Agreement on the customer's part not to store hazardous or illegal property in a box may be included in the contract. Liability for the physical box is standard, since the customer is in effect taking over ownership of it for the rental period.

A signature card is also required. This signature card may be part of the contract, resulting in only one document for record-keeping purposes. Like a NOW, MMIC, or Christmas Club account, access to safe deposit boxes is controlled by signature cards. More than one signature may be required before customer access is allowed, or only one signature may be necessary. How you complete a signature card determines access privileges. We'll talk more about these documents and their importance in *Chapter 11 — Account Ownership.*

When renting a safe deposit box, the bank issues you two keys. These keys are identical. We recommend that they be kept in different places, in case one key is ever lost. After receiving them, most banks ask that you sign a document (perhaps just the empty envelope where the keys were stored) acknowledging receipt. Since each box is physically identified by a number or code, both keys may also reflect this identification.

Will possession of a key allow anyone access to a box?

No! Although the key is important, don't be fooled by the popular misconception that it's all anyone needs to open a box. Every box has a unique lock. Only the two keys issued at rental time fit this lock. Before bank personnel will allow anyone to attempt access, an *access card* must be signed and verified.

Access cards allow bank personnel to compare signatures with the signature card on record. For example, if John Smith and Mary Smith signed the signature card, but their son Charles Smith attempted access, would he be denied? Yes, because his signature is not on record. Only by executing a new signature card which includes Charles Smith can he be allowed access. Furthermore, a new signature card almost always requires approval from all parties included on the previous card.

Once bank personnel is satisfied with signature validity (if there's any question, they may also request that identification be shown), you will be escorted inside the vault where boxes are stored. Along with a lock for individuals' keys, each box has an additional lock. The latter must be unlocked with a *guard key*. Guard keys are controlled by bank personnel only. A bank may have one or more guard keys, depending on the type of lock involved. Since all boxes in a vault may not have been purchased by the bank at the same time, different types of guard locks may be present.

What's our point? We want to assure you that a safe deposit box is secure.

It takes both your key and the guard key to open a box. Neither key can accomplish access independently.

Although the best of precautions may be taken, unfortunately people do lose keys. If only one is lost, you will be charged for a replacement. If both keys are lost, more is involved. Proof of personal identification (i.e., driver's license) will be required. Bank personnel will compare your signature to their records. Once satisfied with the authenticity of your identification, bank personnel will issue an order for the box to be drilled. A locksmith will drill open the box in question. You, the customer, will be charged for this service, along with the cost of a new lock.

Another way to be denied access privileges is to be delinquent in rent. If you do not pay the rental fee, the bank may prevent you from opening the box. This stipulation is usually spelled out in the contract.

Once you are in physical possession of a safe deposit box, banks traditionally offer another nice privacy feature. Rooms may be available for you to use when reviewing the contents of a safe deposit box. No additional charge is involved. Such rooms are totally enclosed so that no one may view your activities. Also, the doors may lock from the inside to further prevent disturbance.

If you do not wish to use a privacy room, another option is usually available. Vaults housing safe deposit boxes typically include pull-out shelves. This is a quick and easy way to put something in a box or take it out without leaving the immediate area.

When renting a safe deposit box, we recommend that you adopt two habits.

1. *Conduct an annual review.* Consider timing this annual review to coincide with the payment due date. Thoroughly examine the contents of your box to ensure that you are familiar with everything stored in it. Remove any documents or articles which are obsolete.

2. *Maintain an inventory.* Inventorying a safe deposit box should go hand-in-hand with conducting an annual review. Keep an ongoing record of any valuables placed in the box. Delete entries from this list when items are removed. Record the date you place the article in the box along with a thorough description of it.

SAFE DEPOSIT BOX LOG

Date	Description
2/ 4/85	20 shares of WAVA Corporation cert. #320
10/23/85	CD #061813 — West Side Bank $10,000 face value matures on 10/23/88 interest rate is 8.5%, payable monthly
11/ 9/85	Deed #4456 house located at 420 Vine Avenue recorded in Kanawha County on 11-2-85

When conducting an annual review, refer to this log. Make two copies of it. Keep one in the box and the other in a secure place somewhere else (store it in your house with other bank documents such as statements).

Some banks furnish you with a pre-printed log. The latter can be especially useful if you store many items in a box. The forms at the end of this chapter, which you may copy for future use, offer examples of more formalized recordkeeping.

Like any other bank product, safe deposit box rentals vary according to location and market conditions. Box sizes also vary. For example, few rural banks offer the larger boxes because they are usually rented by businesses rather than individuals.

Safe deposit boxes provide excellent protection for your valuables and important papers against fire, theft, and loss. Personal property is kept private, yet is easily obtainable. However, since our primary purpose is to help you earn the best possible profits from your bank investments, we offer one piece of advice:

DO NOT KEEP CASH IN A SAFE DEPOSIT BOX.

Keep your cash in movement! Let it earn interest. Storing it in some box will only decrease its value; to keep pace with today's inflation, money must always be invested in a growth instrument.

Safekeeping

Safekeeping services allow you to rely on bank personnel to secure documents. Note that we used the term "documents" rather than "valuables." Banks do not extend this service to include Grandma's ruby necklace or Uncle Joe's silver dollars! Safekeeping services are designed to protect bank transaction papers. Let's use the purchase of government securities as an example.

When transacting such business, negotiable documents will be issued if a buy order is given. Rather than issuing, let's say, a U.S. Treasury Bond to the buyer, a bank may agree to keep the physical bond in its own vault. The customer is then issued a safekeeping receipt which describes the instrument, customer name and other services safekeeping includes. One example of related services is the clipping of coupons for certain government securities. Any document held in safekeeping may be rendered to the buyer when he presents the receipt.

Documents held in safekeeping are the result of bank transactions. Government securities, stocks purchased through discount brokerage services, and certificates of deposit are common examples of such documents. Bank personnel physically house these papers in the bank's vault, issuing the customer a receipt. The bank is responsible for the safety of these instruments. Bank management performs periodic audits to ensure that all items registered for safekeeping are physically there.

Note also that the vault housing the physical documents may be located in the main bank rather than in a branch. Furthermore, many small banks contract with large banks for use of their safekeeping services. Rarely will in-bank generated documents such as CDs be included in this category. However, a small bank may purchase government securities with a larger bank acting as agent. The purchasing bank will be the one to actually retain the physical document if safekeeping services are requested. Why? More than likely, the larger bank has more available vault space. In addition, when the customer chooses to redeem or sell, easier access to the physical document will be available since the agent bank must also handle these transactions. For the customer, the only disadvantage of these arrangements may be a slight delay in getting physical possession of such documents, because the documents may be stored at a site other than where the customer transacts business.

Why do people use safekeeping services?

Safekeeping services are one way to secure some bank-issued documents without renting a safe deposit box. Access by bank personnel to documents held in safekeeping is an important byproduct of this particular service. There are several good reasons why such availability may be advantageous.

For example, let's say you purchase a CD and it comes due during the summer. Perhaps you will be on vacation. Rather than re-arranging your trip, a CD held in safekeeping may be redeemed without your physical presence. By leaving appropriate instructions with your banker, the CD may be cashed in and the proceeds deposited to a specified account or used to purchase another deposit instrument.

Government securities which include coupons may benefit from safekeeping services. The burdensome task of clipping and redeeming coupons is eliminated. Bank personnel will be responsible for coupon handling, automatically crediting customer's designated accounts with the proceeds.

Safekeeping services are typically offered as a free byproduct of other bank services (i.e., CDs, discount brokerage). Basically, safekeeping involves storing instruments in the bank's vault rather than in your own safe deposit box or house safe. Receipts issued from such transactions, however, should be stored in a secure location (i.e., a safe deposit box). These receipts are your personal record of which instruments the bank holds. Furthermore, having these receipts available makes it considerably easier to remove a document from safekeeping.

Finally, safekeeping services allow you to continue conducting certain aspects of banking (i.e., redeeming CDs) in spite of personal illness, travel, or work obligations.

The following pages may be copied for your own personal use. You may wish to ask your copy center to reduce or enlarge them to fit an appropriate notebook.

STOCKS and BONDS

If Lost, Duplicate Certificates are Generally Issued Only on the Posting of a Costly Indemnity Bond, After a Long Waiting Period.

SHARES PAR VALUE	COMPANY	DESCRIPTION KIND, RATE, MATURITY AND CERTIFICATE NUMBERS	DATE ACQUIRED	COST PRICE	

U.S. SAVINGS BONDS

List, in the Same Column, Bonds of Like Registration.
Replacement Takes Time and is a Highly Troublesome Process.

REGISTERED
IN THE NAME(S) OF

BENEFICIARY (IF ANY)

	FACE AMOUNT	DATE OF ISSUE	COST PRICE	DATE DUE	BOND NUMBER
					DATE REDEEMED

LIFE INSURANCE POLICIES

Itemize in Detail. The Loss of a Policy
Usually Results in Delay, Trouble and Expense.

AMOUNT OF INSURANCE	INSURING COMPANY	POLICY NUMBER	PREMIUM DUE DATE & AMOUNT	NAME OF INSURED	BENEFICIARY (Add Contingent Beneficiary if Desired)

OTHER INSURANCE POLICIES

Identify Each. A Prompt and Desirable
Settlement Requires Presentation of the Policy.

AMOUNT OF INSURANCE	PROPERTY OR ITEM INSURED	KIND OF PROTECTION	INSURING COMPANY	POLICY NUMBER	DATE POLICY EXPIRES

VALUABLE BUSINESS & FINANCIAL PAPERS

Keep an Inventory of ALL Your Valuable Papers. The Loss
of Any Might Prove Most Embarrassing or Be Very Costly.

LEASES	INCOME TAX RECORDS		
	FEDERAL YEARS		
	STATE YEARS		
	YEARS		

DEEDS & MORTGAGES	IMPORTANT CANCELLED CHECKS			

TAX RECEIPTS		MISCELLANEOUS
		SAVINGS DEPOSIT BOOKS, PARTNERSHIP ARTICLES, PATENT COPYRIGHT & TRADE MARK PAPERS, BY-LAWS, ETC.

LEGAL DOCUMENTS & AGREEMENTS	

VALUABLE PERSONAL PAPERS & JEWELRY

Make Complete Records. Some of these Items Can Be Replaced
Only With Great Difficulty — Others Cannot Be Replaced At All.

BIRTH CERTIFICATES		JEWELRY	ALSO HEIRLOOMS, RARE COINS & STAMPS, MEDALS, ETC.

MARRIAGE CERTIFICATES			

MILITARY SERVICE DISCHARGE PAPERS		WILLS	

CITIZENSHIP PAPERS		MISCELLANEOUS	
		FAMILY RECORDS, ADOPTION PAPERS, COURT DECREES, DIPLOMAS, PASSPORTS, ETC.	

SOCIAL SECURITY CARDS			
No. - -			
No. - -			
No. - -			
No. - -			
No. - -			
No. - -			
No. - -			

Chapter 11

Account Ownership

I nvestments, just like the home you live in or the clothes you wear, are legally regarded as *property*. So let's define property.

"Property" is anything which may be owned, possessed, used, or disposed of. The right to use property is broader than ownership; you may legally enter into contracts with others to use property which does not belong to them. Property includes not only physical objects such as cars and homes, but also such things as stocks, bonds, and checking accounts.

You've probably, at some time, heard the terms "real" or "personal" property. These two descriptive terms are used to classify property according to its movability. Actually, it's very simple to determine which classification should be used. If something is not movable, it is *real property*. Otherwise, it is *personal property*.

Real Property

Real property consists of land (including the soil itself) and all permanent attachments to the land. Examples of the latter are fences, walls, and timber. Also included in this classification are minerals found under the soil. Water (i.e., lakes, streams) found upon the land also constitutes real property.

Your home is real property, if it, too, is attached to the land. On the other hand, if you live in a camper it is considered personal property, because a camper is very movable.

Personal Property

Personal property includes movable physical objects as well as your personal investments and evidences of debt. This particular classification is further divided into two categories:

1. tangible   2. intangible

Tangible personal property can be seen, touched, and possessed. Common examples are cars, furniture, clothing, and jewelry.

Intangible personal property refers to investments and debts. The legal term for such property is "choses in action." Examples of the latter are stock certificates, bonds, CDs, and IRAs.

Now that we've given you a mini-lesson in property, we want to emphasize one major fact — all property, regardless of whether it is real or personal, shares a common characteristic. Property is always owned. The owner may be an individual, a family, a group of business people, or even a corporation, but some entity owns it.

Discussing property ownership and all the legal ramifications which go along with it could by itself fill an entire book. We are not a legal guide on property. We are an investment guide, so why even discuss property and ownership rights?

Bank accounts are personal property. Therefore, someone must own them. When it comes to investments, there are two forms of ownership.

1. direct ownership
2. representative ownership

What determines which type of ownership you choose?

Personal needs and circumstances are the main decision makers. When you open an account, ownership is established. The signature card shows which names are on an account. They are the only ones legally entitled to moneys in the account. In the case of a safe deposit box, only parties named on the signature card may access the box.

Signature cards not only specify who owns an account, but they also indicate the type of ownership arrangement. Withdrawals from a checking account may require signatures from two people. A corporation appoints people to sign for the company. When someone dies, a fiduciary may open an account to handle the financial affairs of a deceased person's estate.

All of the above illustrates different types of ownerships. Remember the two broad categories we introduced earlier in this chapter? We said there was direct and representative forms of ownership. Within each of these categories, however, exist many different types of accounts.

How names are stated on signature cards indicates the way related documents, such as withdrawal slips in the case of savings accounts, must be signed. In this chapter, we've

SIGNATURE/TERMS/CONDITIONS CARD — INDIVIDUAL(S)

Account No: *000-000-0* Date: *4-30-86*

Account Caption: *JOHN N. DOE OR MARY J. DOE*

Type of Account: *CHECKING*
(Only one per card: Checking; Choice Checking; Free Checking Plus; Prestige Checking; Checkmatic NOW; Money Market Investment Checking; Regular Savings; Ridge Savings; Money Market Savings; Certificate of Deposit)

In consideration of the acceptance and maintenance of this account by The Blue Ridge Bank, N.A. (hereinafter called the "Bank"), the undersigned (whether one or more hereinafter called "Depositor(s)"), jointly and severally agree(s) to the terms and conditions of this contract. Depositor(s) shall be bound by and agree(s) to the Bank's service fees and rules now or hereafter in effect. Depositor(s) hereby acknowledge(s) receipt of a copy of the Bank's Service Charge Schedule. If this account is a Checkmatic NOW account, a Money Market Investment Checking, Prestige Checking, a Regular Savings, a Valley Savings, a Money Market Savings, a Time Deposit or a Certificate of Deposit, Depositor(s) hereby acknowledge(s) receipt of a copy of the Rules and Regulations in effect as of the date hereof.

The Depositor(s), whose signature(s) appears below are authorized to sign checks, drafts, withdrawals or other orders for the payment of funds from this account; and the Bank is hereby authorized to pay such checks, drafts, withdrawals or orders, for part or all of the funds standing to the credit of this account, upon the signature of any one Depositor, including those drawn to the individual order of a signer.

Depositor(s) acknowledge(s) and agree(s) that the additional terms and conditions set forth on the reverse side hereof are a part of this contract.   *MMN-JONES*

AUTHORIZED SIGNATURE OF DEPOSITOR(S):   TAXPAYER IDENTIFICATION NUMBER:

John N. Doe | 1 | 2 | 3 | 4 | 5 | 6 | 7 | 8 | 9 |

Mary J. Doe

NOTICE: SEE REVERSE SIDE FOR IMPORTANT TERMS AND CONDITIONS

TAX INFORMATION CERTIFICATION

Under penalties of perjury, I certify that:
(1) The Taxpayer Identification Number (Social Security Number or Employer Identification Number) appearing in the blocks above is correct and that
(2) I am not subject to backup withholding either because I have not been notified that I am subject to backup withholding as a result of a failure to report all interest and dividends, or because the Internal Revenue Service has notified me that I am no longer subject to backup withholding.

IF YOU ARE SUBJECT TO BACKUP WITHHOLDING, CROSS OUT PART (2) ABOVE

Signature *John N. Doe*   Date *4-30-86*
1/86   410

Multipurpose Signature Card — Front

ADDITIONAL TERMS AND CONDITIONS

1. JOINT ACCOUNT - WITH SURVIVORSHIP. If more than one signature appears on the front of this card, Depositor(s) agree, each with the other and with the Bank, as follows: that all sums now on deposit or hereafter deposited in this account and all interest, if any, thereon shall be owned by them jointly as joint tenants with the right of survivorship, and not as tenants in common, and shall be payable to and may be withdrawn by any of them, or the survivor(s); that any or all sums may be paid by the Bank, without any liability of the Bank to any of the Depositor(s), in accordance with the order of any court; that any depositor(s) may deposit to this account moneys, warrants, checks, drafts and other items belonging to any of the other Depositor(s) and each of said Depositor(s) appoints each of the other Depositor(s) and/or the Bank as attorney in fact to endorse all warrants, checks, drafts and other items payable to the order of any one or more of them, and agrees that Bank is authorized to receive for deposit in said account any and all such items so endorsed, and also such other funds as may be paid the Bank for the account of any or all of them. Each Depositor(s) guarantees to the Bank the genuineness of each of the signatures on the reverse side hereof and agrees that the Bank shall have the right to charge against this account any liabilities at any time existing of any one or more Depositor(s) to the Bank.

2. REOPENED ACCOUNTS. Should this account be closed at any time or times by withdrawal of the balance of the credit thereof, and later reopened by any of the Depositor(s), such reopened account shall be subject to all the terms and conditions of this contract.

3. ITEMS RECEIVED FOR DEPOSIT OR COLLECTION. All checks, drafts and other items received for deposit or collection are accepted by the Bank only as the agent of Depositor(s) for collection only and at Depositor(s) risk, and the Bank assumes no responsibility beyond its exercise of due care. All items are credited subject to final payment and to receipt of final payment in cash or solvent credits by the Bank at its own office and will not be subject to withdrawal until after payment is received by the Bank. Any item may be forwarded through any Federal Reserve Bank for collection or may be presented or sent for collection direct to the payor or drawee or to any correspondent or sub-agent for collection and remittance by cash, bank draft, credits or other customary method of settlement. The Bank shall not be liable for the negligence, insolvency, or other default of any such Federal Reserve Bank, payor, drawee, correspondent or sub-agent, or for loss or delay in the mails or otherwise, and shall have the right to charge back the amount of any item for which final and actual payment is not received, whether or not the item itself can be returned. The Bank may charge back any item drawn on the Bank which is ascertained to be drawn against insufficient funds or otherwise not good or payable.

Multipurpose Signature Card — Back

included examples of the more popular forms of ownership. We've also explained when these various forms are most appropriate.

Okay, we've established that signature cards tell bank personnel who owns an account, but is that the only purpose of this particular document?

No. The signature card is the bank's most effective means of identifying its customers, because the card can be used to compare signatures.

If all parties on the account are not present when the account is opened, most banks will establish a temporary signature card; only those present sign it. A permanent card is established once the remaining parties mail it back or come in to sign it. When transactions are made to an account, particularly withdrawals, bank personnel verify the requestor's signature. It is compared with the signature on the account's card. A few banks in the United States have a computerized verification system. Using a special pen, you actually record your signature in computer files. A sample signature is then requested and compared when a withdrawal is made.

Direct Ownership

Direct ownership accounts are classified as such because they are intended for the customer's own use. The customer has full control over the accounts for individual use or for a special purpose such as an unincorporated business. In some cases (joint tenancy), direct ownership allows more than one owner with each having equal control over the funds.

Popular types of direct ownership accounts are:

- individual
- joint tenancy
- tenancy in common
- special
- proprietorship or trade name
- partnership or trade name

Individual — Just as the name implies, an individual account is held in one name only and is under this person's sole control. Any individual (unless unable to affix his signature) may open such an account. If the owner of an individual account dies, the account's balance accrues to the owner's estate and is distributed by the executor named in the will or by the estate's administrator in the absence of a will.

Mary L. Smith

Mary L. Smith is the sole owner of this account. She is the only one who can access moneys held in the account.

Joint Tenancy — This type of account is opened for two or more persons. Moneys are owned as joint tenants with rights of survivorship. All individuals named may deposit or withdraw funds from the account.

A husband and wife usually open a joint tenancy account. Legally, neither party has exclusive rights to the account. Both are considered to have equal rights. This type of account is also recommended for elderly or infirm persons. In the event one party becomes incapacitated, business can continue.

If one of the owners dies, the account's balance becomes the survivor's property. A bank will normally release all moneys upon presentation of the instrument (if applicable), a signed withdrawal order, a death certificate of the deceased joint tenant and (in most states) an appropriate inheritance tax release. As you can see, one obvious advantage afforded by a joint tenancy account is that funds are transferred to surviving account owners without the expense or delay of probate court proceedings.

Robert K. Smith or
Mary L. Smith

Both Robert K. Smith and Mary L. Smith are recognized as the legal owners of this account. Either person may withdraw all or any part of the funds. The word "or" allows access by either party.

Tenancy in Common — Two or more persons may open a tenancy in common account. These accounts require the signature of all parties before any withdrawals can be made. Some banks no longer offer these types of accounts. They are very restrictive, since all owners must sign for withdrawals. These accounts are usually opened by two or more persons having a sum of money they wish to control together.

If one of the owners dies, the survivors cannot access funds without the consent of the deceased's administrator. The instrument (if applicable) must usually be presented along with a withdrawal order signed by both the survivor and the administrator.

Robert K. Smith and
Mary L. Smith

Both Robert K. Smith and Mary L. Smith are recognized as the legal owners of this account. However, neither person may withdraw moneys without the other's signature. The word "and" requires the signatures of all parties.

Special — Provides for funds to be set aside for a specific purpose. This account may be opened for an individual or two or more persons.

Betty Jones,
Household Account

Betty Jones owns this account. She is using it to deposit moneys related to household expenses.

Proprietorship or Trade Name — Used for business purposes. It is carried in the individual's name or in the business' trade name by the individual.

Joe's Garden Shop
by Joe Williams, Owner

Joe's Garden Shop is a sole proprietorship. Joe Williams has the authority to sign for this account.

Partnership or Trade Name — Two or more individuals may open this type of account in order to conduct business. The account may carry their names or a trade name.

Auto Supply Company,
by Lee Jones or Harry Smith

Lee Jones and Harry Smith own an unincorporated business called Auto Supply Company. Either party may make withdrawals.

CERTIFICATE OF AUTHORITY
for
CORPORATE ACCOUNT

I DO HEREBY CERTIFY that the following is a true copy of a resolution of the Board of Directors of _____ a corporation duly organized and existing under the laws of the State of _____ and having its principal place of business in _____ which resolution was duly adopted at a regular meeting of the said Board, held _____ , 19 _____ a quorum being present, and as set forth in the minute book of said corporation in my custody and control; and that the said resolution has not been rescinded or modified and is not inconsistent with the Charter and By-Laws of the Corporation:

"RESOLVED: That _____ be and hereby is authorized and directed to pay checks, drafts or other orders for the payment of money, drawn on this Corporation, including those drawn to the individual order of a signer, when signed in the following manner.

(Number of signatures required on each instrument) _____

(*Manner of signing) _____

_____

_____ ."

I FURTHER CERTIFY that the following are officers of this corporation having been elected to hold office until their successors are elected:

Chairman of the Board _____

President _____

Vice-President(s) _____

Secretary _____

Assistant Secretary(s) _____

Treasurer _____

Assistant Treasurer(s) _____

WITNESS my hand and the official seal of this corporation this ____ day of _____ , 19_____ .

(SEAL) _____
Secretary

Taken, subscribed and sworn to before me by _____

this _____ day of _____ , 19_____ .

_____
Notary Public

_____ County

My commission expires _____ .

* Give title of officers authorized to sign.

Representative Ownership

Representative ownership is used by an individual or individuals who have written authority to act in another capacity rather than for themselves.

Popular types of representative ownership accounts are:

- corporate
- unincorporated organization
- attorney-in-fact
- fiduciary

Corporate — These accounts are used by corporate officers to conduct business transactions for the corporation. Such officers are sanctioned by the Board of Directors of the incorporated firm to establish and sign on bank accounts.

Ace Corporation

Ace Corporation sanctions certain officers with the right to conduct banking business. These officers must be named in a special document provided to the bank, such as our sample Certificate of Authority for Corporate Accounts.

Unincorporated Organization — Opened to conduct the business of associations, churches, lodges, etc. Any non-profit organization can open this type of account, including federal, state, county and city governments.

These accounts should be titled solely in the name of the organization and not in the name of any individual member or officer of the organization. A resolution certificate by the organization's officers stating who should have withdrawal powers is usually required by the bank.

First Baptist Church of Anytown

First Baptist Church of Anytown authorizes certain individuals with the right to conduct banking business. These individuals must be named in a special document provided to the bank, such as our sample Certificate of Authority for Signatures.

Attorney-in-fact — This type of account is opened when an individual depositor wishes to confer full or limited powers on some other person or persons with respect to the account.

CERTIFICATE OF AUTHORITY
for
SIGNATURES

I DO HEREBY CERTIFY that the following is a true copy of a resolution

of the Governing Body of _____

an organization existing under the laws of the State of _____

and having its principal place of business in _____
which resolution was duly adopted at a regular meeting of the said

Governing Body, held _____, 19____, a quorum being present, and as set forth in the minute book of said organization in my custody and control; and that the said resolution has not been rescinded or modified and is not inconsistent with the Charter and By-Laws of the organization:

"RESOLVED: That _____ be and hereby is authorized and directed to pay checks, drafts or other orders for the payment of money, drawn on this organization, including those drawn to the individual order of a signer, when signed in the following manner:

(Number of signatures required on each instrument) _____

('Manner of signing) _____

_____

_____ ."

I FURTHER CERTIFY that the following are officers of this organization having been elected to hold office until their successors are elected:

Chairman of the Board _____

President _____

Vice-President(s) _____

Secretary _____

Assistant Secretary(s) _____

Treasurer _____

Assistant Treasurer(s) _____

WITNESS my hand and the official seal of this organization this

_____ day of _____ , 19____ .

(SEAL)   _____
                                              Secretary

Taken, subscribed and sworn to before me by _____

this _____ day of _____ , 19____ .

_____
                                            Notary Public

_____ County

My commission expires _____ .

* Give title of officers authorized to sign.

Anyone so authorized is commonly known as an attorney-in-fact. (See sample on page 110.)

A legal document, commonly known as a Power of Attorney, must be given to a bank before this type of account can be opened. This paper names the account holder (also known as the "principal") as well as the person or persons vested with powers (i.e., withdrawals, check endorsements) over the account. The extent of such powers should be specified in the Power of Attorney. Consult your lawyer as to the specifics of this document.

Rights granted under a Power of Attorney are only effective during the principal's lifetime. The depositor's death automatically invalidates any and all rights granted under this document. When the bank receives notification of the depositor's death, the bank can no longer accept the attorney-in-fact's signature in connection with the account.

Henry Jones by
Susan Green, Attorney-In-Fact

Henry Jones is the principal. Moneys deposited in this account are his. Susan Green, however, has been given control over the account through a Power of Attorney. If so specified in this document, she may make withdrawals using only her signature.

Why do people open this type of account?

Frequently, the principal may be unable to act on his own behalf at all times. This may stem from illness, travel, physical residence in another part of the country, etc. The principal may not, however, wish to transfer funds to the person or persons named as attorney-in-fact upon death, thus one reason for choosing an attorney-in-fact account rather than a joint tenancy account. Another reason may be that the principal only wishes to confer these powers for a limited time. For example, a Power of Attorney may be drawn up if someone plans to be out of the country for six months. Once he returns, the document will be revoked.

Fiduciary — Opened for a fiduciary where his capacity and title to the funds are a matter of public record as in a Deed of Agreement, or under a will, or where control of the funds is authorized by court decree, etc.

POWER OF ATTORNEY
(Sample)

I, Robert F. Jones, the undersigned, currently residing at 230 Main Street, Charleston, West Virginia, do hereby make, constitute, and appoint my daughter, Mary L. Jones, my true and lawful attorney in fact to act on my behalf for my use and benefit.

Said power of attorney shall include, but not be limited to, the power to pay all of my lawful debts or any other money coming into my hands, in the form of social security income, retirement income, or from any other source, which said monies are to be deposited in said checking account from which my lawful debts shall be paid.

Said power of attorney shall have the power to exercise any act, power, duty, right, or obligation whatsoever that I now have, or may hereafter acquire the legal right, power or capacity to exercise or perform, in connection with, arising from, or relating to any person, item transaction, business property, real or personal property or matter whatsoever.

This instrument is to be construed and interpreted as a general power of attorney. The enumeration of specific items, rights, acts, and powers herein is not intended to, nor does it, limit or restrict, and is not to be construed or interpreted as limited or restricting, the general powers herein granted to said attorney-in-fact.

The rights, powers, and authorities herein granted shall commence and be in full force and effect upon the signing of this document and shall terminate only upon my death or by my written notice to said attorney-in-fact.

EXECUTED this the _____ day of _____, in Charleston, West Virginia.

_____
Robert F. Jones

STATE OF WEST VIRGINIA
COUNTY OF KANAWHA, to-wit:

I, _____, a Notary Public in and for the county and state aforesaid, do hereby certify that ROBERT F. JONES, whose name is signed to the foregoing writing bearing the date the _____ day of _____, has this day acknowledged same before me in my said county.

Given under my hand this the _____ day of _____.

My commission expires _____

_____
Notary Public

A fiduciary is any person, group or corporation acting in a trust capacity such as trusts, executor, administrator, guardian, conservator, receiver, committee or assignee for a stated principal. A fiduciary differs from an attorney-in-fact. A fiduciary holds title to the account's moneys while the attorney-in-fact does not; the latter acts only for the principal. Also, a fiduciary may be subject to court jurisdiction while an attorney-in-fact is not.

Fiduciaries may receive from the probate court or other court of proper jurisdiction the authority to act on the behalf of deceased persons, incompetents, or minors. Written authorization must be presented to the bank as evidence of the fiduciary's legal capacity to act. This document can vary depending on the situation. As you'll shortly discover, fiduciary accounts can be classified under several different headings.

With the exception of an informal trusteeship, all fiduciary accounts require written authorization from a legal entity before they can be opened. Withdrawals from court-restricted accounts may be made only by parties specified by the particular court of jurisdiction. In some cases, the court will request surety company indemnification for the fiduciary's actions; in such cases, the surety will usually exercise joint control over the account.

Fiduciary accounts may be classified as:

1. decedent estate
2. guardianship
3. committeeship
4. formal trusteeship
5. informal trusteeship
6. custodial

A *decedent estate account* is opened by an authorized person appointed by a court to handle the financial affairs of a deceased person's estate. The executor or administrator does not have any right to delegate authority to any other person. Only those persons who have been properly appointed by the court may act in the handling of estate funds and property. Therefore, an executor may not appoint a co-signer or attorney-in-fact for the purpose of making transactions on the account.

Estate of John R. Smith, deceased,
by Jean C. Smith, Executor

A *guardianship account* is sometimes referred to as an "estate of living persons." These accounts are opened by authorized parties appointed to handle the financial affairs of people judicially determined to be incapable of handling their own finances. The principal (account owner) could be a minor.

The guardian does not have the right to delegate authority to any other person. Only those persons who have been properly appointed by the court may act in the handling of guardianship funds. Therefore, a guardian cannot delegate his or her authority to another person. This account gives the person appointed as guardian a safe method of maintaining records and administering the affairs of someone else.

James B. Green
by Robert M. Green, Guardian

A *committeeship account* is very similar to a guardianship account. It, too, is opened in the principal's name by an authorized person appointed by the courts to handle the principal's affairs. More specifically, however, a committeeship account is used when the principal is an incompetent.

Lee Jones by
Pamela Smith, Committee

A *formal trusteeship account* is one in which an individual or a corporation as trustee has possession of and legal title to a principal's property, but not equitable or beneficial ownership of the property. There are two specific trustee account arrangements:
1. Trust Under Will (testamentary trust)
2. Trust Under Deed (living trust)

As their name implies, one exists after death in accordance with the terms of a will while the other applies during the principal's lifetime.

Trust Under Will (testamentary Trust) — an estate account opened for persons who are acting as trustees under a will.

Mary A. Jones, Trustee
under will of
Betty L. Jones, deceased

Trust Under Deed (living trust) — an account requiring the appointment of a trustee, because of an instrument executed by a living person creating a trust.

Richard D. Smith, Trustee
for Lisa E. Smith under Deed of Trust
of Paul L. Jones dated 3/1/86

An *informal trusteeship account* allows an individual to have funds entrusted by means of an informal agreement. This is the only type of fiduciary account which does not require formal court documents for your bank's files.

Ross Green by
Mark Green

An account opened for a minor is probably the most popular example of an informal trusteeship account. Such accounts are typically opened by a parent or some other relative in trust for a minor child. By the way, these accounts are an excellent way to introduce children to the banking business; they are a great way to encourage the savings habit at an early age.

A *custodial account* is opened for a person legally designated as a representative payee who accepts the responsibility of receiving funds for someone else. Social security payments are a common usage for this fiduciary classification. With a social security custodial account, the representative payee accepts the responsibility of receiving social security benefits for a child, full-time college student (under age 22), or for an adult who is unable to use social security benefits in his own interests.

Ruth Green
by Sharon Green, Custodian

Obviously there are many ways to own a bank account. How the account is titled may vary among banks, but the basic concepts remain the same. Supporting legal documents may also vary, but again the idea is the same.

Sometimes it may be desirable to add or delete names in an account. Most banks will accomodate such requests without requiring you to open a new account.

So what do you do, simply call up the bank and tell them what you want?

It's not quite that simple. To add a name, a new signature card is required. Usually all parties presently signing must re-sign. To remove a name, a new signature card is also required. It should be signed by those parties retaining ownership of the account.

Throughout this chapter, we've emphasized signature cards and how signatures are recorded on them. Why? Because signa-tures are important when it comes to transacting bank busi-ness. However, most bank accounts also require physical evi-dence of ownership. Examples are Certificates of Deposits and savings passbooks.

If you lose these physical documents, can you still withdraw related moneys?

Yes. By signing an affidavit and presenting proof of identity (i.e., driver's license), you can still negotiate the account. Of course, the signature you affix to an affidavit will be compared to that contained on the bank's signature card!

Your bank accounts are properties. When you sign signature cards, you are in fact stating who has legal ownership of this property. Few people ever use any type of ownership besides individual or joint tenancy. Just keep in mind that if special needs do arise, your bank can probably accomodate them.

Chapter 12

The Compounding And Interest Game

W hat are the most misunderstood, confusing aspects of banking?

For the average investor, compounding frequencies, interest methods, and payment frequencies have got to be the most perplexing topics associated with banking. If your goal is to earn the best rates possible on your investments, you must understand what banks are really saying when they advertise interest rates. For instance, the 9% rate paid by XYZ Bank may not be the same as ABC Bank's 9% rate. The "effective annual yield" is what counts!

In previous chapters, we introduced the term "effective annual yield." It refers to the "true" rate your money is earning. What's the basis for calculating this percentage? The "effective annual yield" or rather "true" interest rate being earned is based on rate as well as how frequently interest is compounded.

Let's use a 9% interest rate as an example.

COMPOUNDING TABLE — 9% RATE

annually — 9.000%
quarterly — 9.308%
monthly — 9.381%
weekly — 9.409%
daily — 9.416%

Depending on compounding frequency, a 9% rate can yield anywhere from 9% to 9.416%. As your balance grows, naturally this earnings gap becomes more evident. For example, on a

$1,000 balance this difference will net you only $4.16 annually; however, on a $50,000 balance you'll see an annual difference of $208.

In order to understand interest rates and their relationship with compounding frequencies, you first have to realize that the amount of interest paid may be calculated in a variety of ways. Different concepts of interest exist. And it's legal for banks to subscribe to different philosophies. Competition, rather than regulation, is usually what keeps most of the banks in your town alike when it comes to compounding.

Interest can either be earned or paid. Since we're concentrating on the investment aspects of banking, naturally our emphasis is on interest earned.

Interest Earned — Interest earned is the amount a financial institution pays you for keeping certain deposits with them. Just as you pay a bank interest to borrow money (i.e., car loans), a bank must also pay to borrow funds.

Interest is defined one of two ways — *simple* or *compound.*

Simple — Interest is not added to the account's balance for the purpose of compounding.

Compound — Interest is added to the account's balance when due (i.e., daily, monthly) and thereafter made to bear interest. This is commonly referred to as "interest on interest."

Obviously if an on-going account is involved (i.e., checking, savings), interest must eventually be compounded even if your bank subscribes to the "simple" concept. Can you imagine having a savings account for 10 years and never receiving the benefit of any interest which had been earned. That would be ludicrous! If a maturity type instrument is involved (i.e., CD), interest may never be compounded; in such cases, simple interest may be paid at term.

Generally when an account is earning simple interest, you can infer that such interest will be compounded annually. Thus, 9% simple interest has an effective annual yield of 9%.

How often do you hear the term "daily interest" when listening to, or reading bank ads?

Pretty often.

Is "daily interest" the same as "daily compounding?"

No. Unfortunately, not everyone understands the difference. We say "unfortunately" because this lack of understanding can be costing you money.

Compounding, you will recall, occurs when interest is added to the balance of your account so that it can begin earning interest also. On the other hand, such terms as "daily interest" refer to interest calculation methods.

Daily Interest — A method of computing interest in which the depositor earns interest on money from the day it's deposited until the day it's withdrawn. This method is also known as "day-of-deposit-to-day-of-withdrawal interest."

"Daily interest" considers the actual number of days in any given period. For example, it recognizes that there are 31 days in the month of July. A 365-day year (unless it's Leap Year) is used. Some banks, however, base earnings on a 360-day year. In these cases, true "daily interest" is not paid. (Ask your banker what year base is used — 360 or 365.) Calculations based on a 360-day year assume that every month consists of 30 days.

Other concepts applicable to the calculation of interest include:

Average Balance — The average daily balances maintained throughout an interest period are used as the base for computing interest.

$$\frac{S}{D} \times R = \text{interest earned}$$

S = sum of daily balances for period
D = number of days in period
R = interest rate for period

Low Balance — Interest is computed using the account's minimum balance during a stated period of time.

$$LB \times R = \text{interest earned}$$

LB = low balance for period
R = interest rate for period

FIFO — FIFO is an acronym for "first in, first out." Interest is paid from the day of deposit until the end of the earning's period. When adjusting interest to consider withdrawals, the latter are subtracted from the earliest deposits made. Thus, the accrued interest loss caused by withdrawals may be relatively high when FIFO is used.

LIFO — LIFO is an acronym for "last in, first out." Interest is paid from the day of deposit until the end of the earning's period. When adjusting interest to consider withdrawals, the latter are subtracted from the last deposits made.

Which of the above methods offer you the best deal?

Usually the daily-interest method nets you the most, particularly if withdrawals are made.

While discussing interest calculations, we've repeatedly referred to "the earnings period," the length of time when interest is being calculated for the purpose of payment.

Interest can be paid at various times. An earnings period can consist of a month, quarter, etc. Payment frequencies vary according to the type of account involved and bank policy. Once interest is paid, it's available for customers to access; it can be left on deposit or withdrawn.

Payment frequency attains a somewhat greater degree of importance when simple interest is paid rather than the more attractive daily compounding. CDs provide an excellent example. An instrument earning simple interest might pay interest monthly if you so request. This money can in turn be deposited to another interest-bearing account such as an MMIC. In a sense, you've managed to compound the money — the interest is now available to earn interest.

In brief, the way your bank pays interest consists of the following considerations:

1. when interest is credited to the balance — (compounding frequency)
2. what type of balance is used — (calculation method — daily interest, FIFO, LIFO, etc.)
3. when interest is paid — (payment frequency — monthly, quarterly, etc.)

People typically confuse items #1 and #3. When interest is credited to the account's balance and when it is actually paid are two different subjects. For example, a bank may compound interest daily, but only pay it monthly. And daily interest isn't the same as daily compounding. When shopping for interest rates, check out the following:

1. compounding frequency
2. calculation method
3. payment frequency

Other considerations can also influence how much interest you will earn. Examples are minimum balance requirements and service charges. Multi-tiered rates are used by some banks.

Balance	Earnings Rate
$0 - $ 999.99	6.361%
$1,000.00 - $2,499.99	7.250%
$2,500.00 - $4,999.99	7.861%
$5,000.00 and greater	8.722%

Regardless of the instrument involved, find out how interest earnings are calculated and credited. Interest isn't just a matter of percentages. Learn how to decipher what bankers mean when they quote rates. Methods subscribed to by competing institutions can make or cost you extra profits. As we said earlier, not every 9% rate is identical!

The IRS Connection

T he interest you earn on bank deposits is taxable at the federal level. It may also be taxable at state and local levels.

The above rule is fairly constant year in and year out. There have been rare exceptions such as a special All Saver's Certificate popular a few years ago. Congress allowed interest exclusions of $200 (single) and $400 (married) one year. However, as a rule of thumb every cent you earn on bank deposits must be considered when figuring your taxes. Government securities, on the other hand, usually afford you some tax relief, at least on the state and local levels.

Our emphasis in this chapter is bank deposits (i.e., NOWs, MMICs, CDs) and what the Internal Revenue Service demands. To begin with, you should realize that interest must be reported. A failure to do so can cost you penalties as well as the taxes owed. Tax evasion and falsification can even result in a prison term.

It's *illegal* to skip reporting interest to the IRS. You must report it, and you must pay taxes if applicable.

With more than 50,000 banks and branches in the United States (not counting S&Ls and other such financial institutions), how does the IRS know the amount of interest you've earned?

Federal regulations require banks and other such financial institutions to report all interest payments to the IRS. This is largely accomplished by the use of computers.

"But look how many people have the same name. How does the IRS know which John E. Smith received the interest?"

In case the above question just happened to cross your mind, the answer (when individuals are involved) is Social Security Numbers (SSNs). Everyone who has an SSN should have a unique number. If there are 36 John E. Smiths in your town, each should have a unique SSN. When you file your income tax papers, you *must* include your SSN. When a bank reports how much interest has been paid to a specific account, they also report the SSN attached to the account. Thus, the IRS can match up your papers with bank records and then determine whether you are accurately reporting interest earnings.

Beginning in 1984, a new law went into effect nationwide enforcing stricter requirements for reporting interest. The Interest and Dividend Tax Compliance Act of 1983 stipulated that recipients of interest or dividend income are subject to certain IRS penalties and the withholding of taxes at a 20% rate from their interest and dividend payments if they fail to furnish payers (i.e., banks, S&Ls) with a correct Taxpayer Identification Number (TIN). This withholding stipulation is commonly referred to as Backup Withholding.

Note that we've suddenly started using the term "Taxpayer Identification Number" rather than SSN. If individuals are involved, the Taxpayer Identification Number is the SSN. If corporations or other organizations own the account, the Employers Identification Number (EIN) serves as the Taxpayer Identification Number. Even informal organizations, such as garden clubs and softball leagues, must furnish a TIN or be subject to Backup Withholding.

What if you've never worked and don't have a TIN?

You can apply for a TIN by contacting your local Social Security Administration Office or the IRS. Complete form SS-5 for an SSN or form SS-4 for an EIN.

Now let's talk about Backup Withholding.

Backup Withholding is a federal regulatory provision which affords the IRS with a tax collection method for interest and dividend income. Should Backup Withholding apply to your accounts, the institution paying you interest will forward the withheld amount to the U.S. Treasury. Backup Withholding does not represent any additional or new form of taxation; all amounts withheld are fully allowable tax credits against your total income tax liability when returns are filed.

Under what circumstances will Backup Withholding be enforced?

1. The payer does not have your correct TIN on file.
2. The IRS notifies the payer that you have furnished an incorrect TIN.
3. When opening a new account after December 31, 1983, you fail to certify under penalties of perjury that the TIN furnished is correct.

4. When opening a new account after December 31, 1983, you fail to certify under penalties of perjury that you are not subject to Backup Withholding.

5. The IRS notifies the payer that you have previously underreported taxable income and withholding must begin.

In addition to 20% Backup Withholding, other IRS penalties may apply if incorrect TINs are used or if interest is not reported. The IRS can assess a $50 penalty if you fail to furnish a correct TIN. A $500 penalty along with criminal charges may be incurred if you make a false statement to avoid withholding. A 5% penalty may be charged on underreported interest payments.

Is anything or anyone exempt?

Yes. Examples are IRAs and real estate investment trusts. When you establish an account with a bank, they should ask you to certify a TIN and tell you whether the account is subject to Backup Withholding. Accounts opened prior to January 1, 1984, which are subject to this provision should have been certified in late 1983. Most banks made special mailings to their customers explaining what was happening and asked for confirmation of TINs already on file.

Errors can happen, however, and sometimes Backup Withholding is erroneously applied to an account. If it is caused by a false or missing TIN, furnish your bank with a correct number (certified under penalties of perjury) to stop the withholding. But if Backup Withholding is the result of your underreporting interest payments, the bank is legally required to withhold money until otherwise notified by the IRS.

Although such government issues as U.S. Savings Bonds and T-bills are exempt from state and local taxes, they too must reflect your current TIN. When redeeming such instruments, you must furnish a TIN. When purchasing new securities such as T-bills or T-bonds, you are required to furnish a TIN so as to avoid Backup Withholding on interest payments.

This tax law further provides that 1099 forms or other statements issued in lieu of them be mailed to everyone receiving interest payments subject to taxation. These mailings reflect interest paid through December 31 of each year. The amounts

---

*Payer in all of the above refers to the institution paying the interest (i.e., bank, S&L, credit union).

reflected on such documents should agree with the amounts your bank has reported to the IRS. In case of errors, you must notify the bank *immediately*.

We've repeatedly emphasized that interest must be reported to the IRS using a correct TIN. But what if different people own an account and interest payments are so divided?

More than one person can own an account. This may be done for a number of reasons. Perhaps you are related to the other person. You may belong to an informal investment club (just a bunch of neighbors). Better interest rates may be possible by combining funds to achieve larger balances.

The reasons are endless. What we're concerned with is how you report the interest.

An account reflects only one TIN. If three people are involved and they do not represent a partnership or corporation (in such cases, EINs are used), only one of them will be viewed by the IRS as receiving interest from the account.

Let's say the account earned $3,000 for the taxable year. The person whose SSN was used now has a tax liability of $3,000. If that one person actually received and kept the money, then that tax report is fine. But if all three people split the money three ways, the tax liability should also be split accordingly.

A "Nominee/Middleman 1099" form may be used to report interest belonging to another person. In the case of husband and wife, nominee reporting is not required. If you will look at the back of a 1099-INT form, nominee reporting is usually explained along with all applicable guidelines.

The *nominee* is the recipient of interest paid whose Taxpayer Identification Number is shown on the 1099-INT form. To divide the tax liability, the nominee must file a nominee form with the IRS to show the proper distribution of interest payments. Such forms can be obtained from your local IRS office or most public libraries. On the Form 1096 (Annual Summary and Transmittal of U.S. Information Returns), check the box for "INT" under "Nominee/Middleman 1099s." Along with a Form 1096, the recipient whose TIN was used for tax reporting must complete another 1099-INT form to be filed with the IRS. This revised form shows the amount received after distribution. 1099-INTs must also be supplied to all parties receiving a share of the interest, to inform them of their tax liability.

Chapter 14

Can You Earn Too Much Interest?

I t's great to put your dollars to work earning interest income. What easy money! The only labor on your part is sound decision making.

It's 100% profit, right? WRONG. Never make the mistake of believing that interest income is free money. If you do, the tax collectors are liable to put you behind bars.

In *Chapter 13 — The IRS Connection*, we concentrated more on the bank's responsibility in reporting interest income. Now we're going to discuss your personal responsibilities as an investor. Not every accounting aspect of investment income is automatically handled by your bank.

As we've stated before, interest earned on most deposit instruments sold by banks is taxable at both the federal and state levels. In some situations, such as T-bills, interest earnings are taxable only at the federal level. Interest-bearing checking accounts, CDs, passbook savings, Christmas Clubs and other common investments held by consumers result in extra income which you must report on both federal and (in most cases) state tax returns. Depending on where you live, some of you may also have to report this income to local tax authorities.

Our tax systems are built around the idea of withholding taxes as income is earned. Look at your pay stub. Every time you receive pay, moneys are deducted from federal, state, and local (if applicable) taxes. Our government doesn't depend on your making such remittances. The company you work for deducts these moneys and credits them to your accounts with the proper tax authorities.

This "pay-as-you-go" system does have advantages. To you, the consumer, it eliminates big tax bills at the end of each year.

As to government bodies, this system simplifies the tax collection process. For the most part, it's automatic. Furthermore, this "pay-as-you-go" system keeps dollars flowing into the tax coffers on a steady basis.

Every time you get a raise, more money is withheld for taxes. (The only exception is if taxes are lowered through legislation.) Moneys received as interest income, however, are not reduced by tax deductions; only if backup withholding is in effect will tax payments be automatically subtracted from interest earnings.

You are responsible for reporting interest income and making any additional tax payments. Failure to do so can result in penalties or even a jail sentence.

As we said earlier, most deposit products marketed by banks earn income subject to taxation on all levels. So-called "dividends" paid by credit unions and S&Ls is actually interest income when it comes to taxes. A lot of people, though, don't realize that gifts issued by financial institutions may also be regarded as income by tax authorities.

It wasn't always this way; a gift used to be just a gift. Now anything worth more than a nominal value (that means just about anything more valuable than a box of matches!) will probably be included on the year-end interest statement rendered by your bank. For example, if you receive a calculator valued at $15 for opening a CD, then your year-end interest statement for that CD will probably reflect an extra $15 besides any interest earned. That free calculator, in other words, isn't totally free. Its value represents taxable income. Some banks will even give you a trip to Disney World for opening a large, long-term CD! That's great, as long as you realize that the value of this very nice trip represents taxable income.

How can you determine whether a gift will be taxed?

So you won't be in for a rude awakening when you get that year-end interest statement, ask the bank. You may not want a telescope if it represents extra taxable income! Our point is to make you aware that gifts aren't always as free as they appear to be. In fact, if you carefully read the promotional ads, you'll probably find a notation stating that a gift's value is regarded as interest income to the individual who owns the account.

Now that we've established the potential taxability of interest income, what about the other side of the coin. Can interest reduce your income?

Yes. An interest penalty can be deducted from taxable income. When you forfeit interest, you are in fact losing income.

Along with reporting interest earnings, banks also annually supply you with forfeiture information.

Notice how we've repeatedly said that banks supply you with interest-related figures?

Federal law requires that banks supply both the IRS and individuals with interest income reports on an annual basis. The reports you receive as a consumer may be specially designed statements or 1099 forms. These documents are rendered as of December 31 each year. Your social security number is what identifies your tax records to the government's computers. This number will be found on your individual tax returns, W-2s, and interest statements. Actually any document pertaining to income earned or lost should include your social security number. In the case of a business, the EIN (employer's identification number) is used.

How is interest income reported on tax forms?

Changes in tax laws can naturally change reporting guidelines. Interest exclusions may even be in effect some years. By this we mean that a certain amount of your interest income (such as the first $100) is not subject to taxation. The only sure way to successful tax reporting is to thoroughly study the tax guides. Federal, state, and local authorities all provide you with telephone numbers for additional free assistance.

Make sure the right forms are used. For example, federal forms currently include the 1040EZ, 1040A, and 1040. Not everyone can use any of these three forms. Interest income is one of the key decision points when selecting the right form for an individual. If you make over $400 in interest, you must file a Form 1040. A Schedule B must also be attached, itemizing by source and amount each institution from which you received interest income.

Deposit instruments such as T-bills, U.S. Savings Bonds, and IRAs also influence which tax forms are appropriate. Another key factor is the question, "how much did you pay in estimated taxes?".

Estimated tax is the method people use to pay taxes on income that is not subject to withholding. This income includes interest, dividends, and capital gains. Failure to file estimated tax returns (Form 1040-ES) may result in penalties.

All you are really doing is implementing withholding for income not otherwise subject to it. Payments can be made quarterly or annually. If the payment is large and it's difficult to accurately project income, we recommend the quarterly method.

When filing a 1040, all estimated tax payments are accounted for. The latter are added to any taxes withheld by employers so as to reduce the amount owed. Estimated tax systems may also be in effect on state or local levels.

Can you earn too much interest?

No, as long as you remember that interest earned on most deposit instruments is taxable income. Keep in mind that your friendly neighborhood bank is reporting all those wonderful interest checks to the IRS. With the hi-tech explosion fueled by today's sophisticated computer systems, it's easy for the IRS to match up your social security number with interest earned anywhere in the United States.

Our best advice is:

- Always maintain thorough records of any interest income earned.
- Compare year-end statements issued by financial institutions with your own records. In case of discrepancies, notify the bank as quickly as possible.
- Keep current with tax laws. Carefully read the appropriate booklets each year. Make sure you use the current form.
- Last, but certainly least, be honest when it comes to reporting taxable income to the IRS.

Chapter 15

Banks and S&Ls: Are They Really So Different?

A re banks and S&Ls really so different? At one time they were, but not anymore. Later in this chapter, we'll give you some background material on the origins of S&Ls and how they once differed quite noticeably from banks. But first we want to make sure you understand that the financial marketplace isn't limited to just banks and S&Ls. In fact, when we use the term "bank" we're actually using a word badly in need of an exact descriptor, because there are different types of banks.

Commercial banks are at the center of our financial system. These banks and the services they offer have been the focus of this book. They are by far the most widespread and popular financial institution. They serve as depositories for the funds of individuals, government bodies, and business establishments. They also play major roles in payments functions such as facilitating check clearing and the transfer of funds throughout the United States. Through their lending and investment activities, commercial banks make funds available to individuals, government bodies, and business establishments.

Commercial banking activity can be summarized as consisting of three functions:

1. receive deposits
2. handle payments
3. make loans

The commercial bank is the oldest type of financial institution in the United States. Until the 20th century, however, commercial banks were regarded as financiers of trade and commerce, not as providers of long-term funds for individuals. Many were not engaged in mortgage lending. Under the

National Banking Act of 1863, national banks were actually prohibited from making mortgage loans. For all practical purposes, they catered to the financial needs of business and industry exclusively.

The original concept behind commercial banks ignored financial needs of the average consumer. These institutions did not actively solicit his savings nor did they provide him with a means to purchase homes. As our economy grew, so, too, did the people's financial demands. Individuals, like companies, also needed a place where they could deposit savings and borrow funds. To meet such needs, other financial institutions besides commercial banks were created. Both S&Ls and mutual savings banks were designed to meet the general public's financial needs. We'll talk more about both of these institutions later in this chapter.

Now, our present-day commercial bank does an excellent job of catering to the average person's needs. The term "full-service bank" that many use in their ad campaigns is an ideal description. They cash checks, offer a wide assortment of savings plans, make all types of loans (i.e., car, home improvement, mortgage), offer credit cards, and sell government securities to name but a few of the attractive services and products marketed by today's most popular financial institution — the commercial bank.

Today, many of these institutions also have Trust Departments. Another area where many are active involves correspondent banking. In brief, what this entails is helping other banks with services such as safekeeping of securities, loan participations, funds transfers, etc. More than likely your neighborhood bank isn't a totally independent business. Just as you need certain financial services, banks too often need one another. Perhaps a major corporation needs to borrow $5 million dollars. Although the company is an excellent credit risk, the loan is too large for your neighborhood bank. By working together, two or more commercial banks may participate in a loan agreement which will enable this corporation to obtain adequate funds. International banking is another specialized function that commercial banks in major United States cities are often active in. Overseas handling of funds for individuals, governments, and businesses are managed by these departments. Loans to foreign governments are part of the International Banking scene.

In describing the modern commercial bank, we have explained the main business of any financial institution. Although their charters for doing business and the state or federal regulations which govern them varies, the idea of financial institutions was founded on a single premise.

A financial institution is a channel between savers and borrowers.

Remember the three major commercial banking functions?

1. receive deposits
2. handle payments
3. make loans

True, we went on to explain how commercial banks may also play active roles in trusts, correspondent banking activities, and international banking; but they can offer such services only because they comply with special regulations. The bank must obtain government-issued charters before it is legally authorized to pursue some of these specialized endeavors. In essence, those three basic functions we listed make up the banking business. They link savers with borrowers.

A commercial bank is traditionally regarded as the least specialized financial institution. There are several thousand commercial banks in the United States. While there is great variation in size, most of them are small and independently owned by local people who have purchased stock. The United States is unique in the number of individual banks doing business. While we may be able to pick and choose from several thousand commercial banks, the citizens of Canada have only about a dozen to select from.

A commercial bank may be state or nationally chartered. By the way, you can't just wake up one morning and decide you're going to open a commercial bank. Try it and you might be spending that night in jail! In spite of deregulation, banking is still different from other types of business. It is still more heavily governed by both federal and state laws. And one of these regulations requires a government-issued charter before any business can be transacted. We won't bore you with all the requirements for obtaining a charter, but, take our word, this process is designed to insure that your bank's owners are running an honest, financially sound business.

If the name of your bank contains the word NATIONAL or the abbreviation N.A. (National Association), you are dealing with a nationally chartered commercial bank; otherwise, it is a state bank. Both are governed by federal regulations. Both are subject to periodic examinations for the purpose of insuring that the bank is a financially sound institution. Remember how every now and then you hear about one closing? They probably failed an examination. Periodic exams by highly trained personnel is one way the government guarantees the safety of your deposits. Commercial banks are owned by stockholders — people just like you. Many institutions have been in business for decades, some for longer than 100 years.

Next to commercial banks, the most popular financial institutions are S&Ls. S&L is an abbreviation for Savings & Loan Association. Initially they were organized so that depositors could invest their funds to provide for home financing. S&Ls were a good way for Americans to build up their local communities.

The idea behind S&Ls started in January 1831 at Frankford, Pennsylvania (this area is now part of Philadelphia). History tells us that the idea was developed by six men who met in Sidebotham's Tavern. They were neighbors interested in saving money and stimulating thrift. These six men also wanted to provide funds which would enable them and others like them to buy homes.

The Oxford Provident Building Association was the result of their meeting. In April 1831 the Association made its first loan. Comly Rich, a lamplighter, borrowed $375 in order to buy a home.

Truly phenomenal growth for S&Ls came after the end of World War II. During the 1960s they constituted an industry of over $140 billions in assets. Their growth rate in the years following World War II far exceeded that of commercial banks.

S&Ls may also be called building and loan associations. As we said earlier, S&Ls were organized to attract savings for the primary purpose of making real estate loans. Until recent years, there was a more obvious separation between commercial banks and S&Ls. When interest rates on savings deposits were still highly regulated, the government offered these associations a competitive edge. At one time S&Ls could (if they chose to) pay slightly higher interest rates on savings and time deposits than commercial banks. Why did federal regulators afford them this advantage?

Only in recent years have S&Ls been allowed to enter certain areas of the financial scene. For example, they were unable to offer checking accounts. The government equalled out this difference, in part, by letting S&Ls pay rates ¼ to ½ percentage points above commercial banks.

Today, there is a much finer line between commercial banks and S&Ls. Both can offer checking accounts. Deregulation is making interest rates more a matter of competition rather than regulation. S&Ls are no longer just in the real estate loan business; they are actively making other types of loans (i.e., car, personnel, recreational vehicles). some institutions, however, do limit their lending activity to the real estate market. Realize, though, that is corporate policy, not law.

One of the more noticeable differences involves repayment of funds. Repayment of funds can be stretched out more with S&Ls than with commercial banks. Under their charters, most S&Ls can legally delay repayment of deposits for extended periods. In practice though, they rarely require any notice, paying on demand instead.

S&Ls may be state or federally chartered. Most are owned by depositors; some may issue stock. The vast majority, however, are referred to as mutual companies. In other words, the association is owned by the people who put their savings into the association; these people then elect a board of directors.

Is money deposited in an S&L insured by a reputable body?

Yes, if it is insured by the FSLIC. Check with any S&L you do business with to see if such coverage is available. More about the FSLIC later in this chapter.

Commercial banks and S&Ls are the two most popular financial marketplaces for the average consumer. Both can be found anywhere in the United States. Both do business with the general public. However, there are other entities actively competing for consumers' dollars.

Credit unions are non-profit cooperative associations composed of depositors commonly referred to as "members." Members must have something in common. Frequently a current or former employer is the connecting thread. Many cities have teachers' credit unions. Fraternal and religious organizations sometimes organize credit unions for their members.

Members can both deposit funds and borrow money. One person's savings finance another's credit needs. Such credit needs are usually short-term obligations. Some credit unions, though, have expanded into the mortgage market. Other services recent years have seen (especially for larger ones) include check-like privileges and the opening of more convenient locations.

When you belong to a credit union, it is said that you purchase shares. What you are doing, in fact, is making deposits. Certificates are hardly ever issued. A passbook or other recordkeeping document is usually substituted. Interest earned is referred to as dividends.

Credit unions are controlled by their depositors. members elect a board of directors. This board in turn chooses officers to manage the credit union. Volunteers may also be used to help manage day-to-day activities. In the case of a company credit union, the company may provide free office space and supplies.

There are approximately 20,000 credit unions in the United States. They may be state or federally chartered. All net income resulting from the operation of a credit union is paid out to members or added to its reserves.

Because these institutions have never been as regulated as commercial banks or S&Ls, credit unions can pay higher interest rates on deposits. Before deregulation, rate differences were more noticeable. Today with the many deposit plans offered by most commercial banks and S&Ls, the interest rate gap hardly exists.

Are funds held in credit unions safe?

Check out your credit union to see if it's federally insured. If it is, your deposits are very safe. We'll be talking more about insurance and how it relates to your savings later in this chapter and specifically in *Chapter 16 — Insurance — How Important Is It?*

The *mutual savings bank* is another type of financial institution founded during the early years of America's banking industry. Like the S&L, they too were designed to cater to individuals rather than the business community. Unlike the S&L whose main purpose was to encourage home loan growth, the mutual savings bank's main purpose was to provide individuals with a safe place to deposit savings. The dawn of the 19th century brought with it the Industrial Revolution. As it swept through the United States, the Industrial Revolution created a need for factories, transport systems, and housing requirements for a rapidly growing industrial urban population.

People also began to accumulate more money than they needed for everyday living expenses. Yet the average person lacked a safe place where small accumulations from wages could be placed. Safety and easy availability of savings became a growing concern.

To satisfy these needs, groups of citizens (including several leading commercial bankers of the day) established mutual savings banks. They were copied from similar institutions located in Great Britain. In 1816 the first two such institutions opened for business — The Philadelphia Saving Fund Society and the Provident Institute for Savings in Boston.

Still found primarily in the Northeast, mutual savings banks are always state chartered. They offer services which are typically associated with the savings departments of modern-day commercial banks. Mortgage loans constitute their prime lending activity.

Mutual savings banks are owned by their depositors. There are no stockholders. Policies are set by self-perpetuating boards of trustees (i.e., the original board members select their own successors).

Interest is usually paid in the form of dividends. Legal requirements pertaining to the amounts paid differ from state to state. Mutual savings banks usually subscribe to federal insurance. Check with each institution that you're considering doing business with to see if it's federally insured.

Insurance companies also compete for your savings. Although they are not in the true sense of the word a "savings institution," nevertheless some sell policies which can earn you interest. They also compete in financing business credit needs and are an important secondary mortgage holder.

Another player in the personal investment game is *pension funds*. Pension funds help us insure better retirement income. Your company may offer a plan whereby both the employee and the employer make contributions to such funds. Pension contributions which may be automatically deducted from wages is a long-term investment program popular with countless Americans. Assets comprising pension funds usually consist of stocks and bonds. Legislation in recent years has done much to better scrutinize the safety of these funds.

Mortgage banking companies cater to the borrower rather than the investor. These institutions specialize in buying and selling government-backed mortgages. Examples are FHA and VA loans. They originate mortgage loans and sell them to other investors such as life insurance companies. Loans may be originated in one area of the United States and then sold to an investor located in another physical area.

Mortgage banking companies may also service the loans they make. What do we mean by "servicing?" Servicing involves billing customers, receiving payments, seeing that adequate homeowners' insurance is carried, collecting past due accounts, etc.

Consumer credit companies are often referred to as *finance companies*. They specialize in lending small amounts of money to individuals. People who borrow from finance corporations are generally unable to secure such credit from other institutions. Because these loans are believed to be riskier, interest rates charged are typically higher than those found elsewhere. On the other hand, depositors may also earn higher rates.

If you bank with a consumer credit company, are your deposits insured?

Perhaps by a private insurance company, but never by the federal government. If you choose to invest your savings in a consumer credit company, make sure you understand if and how funds are insured against company default.

What a financial supermarket investors have to shop in!

Although the above institutions number among the older, better known types, there is a new breed gaining momentum. Money market funds are sold by brokerage houses nationwide. Major retail chains such as Sears are competing for your dollars. Even some grocery stores have gotten into the act by introducing financial service centers.

Confusing, right?

It can be for the novice.

Our best advice is:

1. Make sure your deposits are adequately insured.
2. Are funds easily accessible in case of personal emergencies?
3. Will the financial institution meet all or at least most of your banking needs? It can sometimes be advantageous to do all of your financial business with one institution. For example, a bank may give you a better rate on a car loan if you maintain a checking account with them.
4. Know what type of institution you are doing business with. Understand what it can and can't do for you.

Did you notice how the term "regulation" crept into our discussion less frequently as we journeyed through America's most popular financial institutions?

Regulation takes two forms. There are regulations governing interest rates, lending limits, etc. Then there is the regulation of supervisory bodies.

Financial entities such as Sears and consumer credit companies experience neither form of regulation as much as banks and S&Ls do. Since our main topic throughout this book has been the commercial bank, let's take a few pages to highlight how these institutions are regulated.

First of all, why did anyone bother to establish regulatory bodies?

It helped to ensure the safety of your deposits. Stockholders, too, are better protected since regulation encourages management of a stable, financially secure company. Before the Great Depression and the ensuing record-breaking number of bank failures, our government paid little heed to how safe a bank was.

Modern-day banks are primarily supervised by three federal agencies. These agencies are:

1. The Comptroller of the Currency
2. Federal Reserve System
3. Federal Deposit Insurance Corporation (more commonly referred to as the FDIC)

In addition, each state supports regulatory bodies. States may also pass laws which affect bank operations. These laws may deal with such aspects as interest calculations for loans or the opening a new branches.

The Comptroller of the Currency plays a major role in supervising nationally chartered banks. This agency approves applications for charters, mergers, and branches. It examines national banks, using highly trained professionals who specialize in this function. A national bank must be examined twice every three years it is open for business. Examinations may be scheduled even more frequently if there is any indication of problems.

How does the Comptroller's office become aware of any potential problems in between exams?

A nationally chartered bank must file a report of condition three times each year with the Comptroller's office.

It can be said that the Federal Reserve System formulates and executes monetary policy. By establishing reserves, this agency influences how much money is available for credit. The term "reserves" refers to how much money a bank must withhold from its activities. For example, if the Federal Reserve decrees a 12% reserve policy, then 12% of all funds on deposit must be isolated. You could say that the Federal Reserve System forces member banks to save a specified amount of money.

Did you notice how we used the term "member banks?"

Not every bank belongs to this system. Created by Congress in 1913 in response to the numerous bank failures which occurred at the turn of the century, the Federal Reserve System is made up of 12 regional banks. These "banker's banks" service member banks and their branches.

Check clearing and collection is greatly facilitated by the 12 regional banks. Both national and state banks may choose to be members. Although the Federal Reserve does retain examination rights over member banks, exams are usually not performed on state-chartered banks. State banks are typically reviewed by a state-controlled supervisory body similar to the Comptroller's office.

FDIC examiners may also audit banks. *Chapter 16 — Insurance — How Important Is It?* discusses this agency in depth. Remember how people lost their life savings when some of the banks failed during the Great Depression? At that time, an agency like the FDIC didn't exist. The only insurance people had for the safety of their deposits was the trust they placed in bank management and owners. Today, much more insurance is offered. Regardless of how poorly your bank is managed, if it's insured by the FDIC, then you're guaranteed withdrawal of funds up to $100,000 even if the bank fails.

BANK REGULATORY AUTHORITIES

Type of Commercial Bank	Regulatory Authority
National	Comptroller of the Currency Federal Reserve System FDIC
State banks that are members of the Federal Reserve System	State regulatory body Federal Reserve System FDIC
State banks that are not members of the Federal Reserve System but are insured by the FDIC	State regulatory body FDIC
State banks that are not members of the Federal Reserve System but are not insured by the FDIC	State regulatory body

What about money deposited in an S&L?

The Federal Savings and Loan Insurance Corporation (known as the FSLIC) guarantees accounts up to the $100,000 limit.

Other regulatory bodies besides the three we've just highlighted also exist.

The Department of Justice regulates bank mergers to avoid monopolies. The Securities and Exchange Commission requires banks to file regular, detailed reports since stock trading activity exists. Banks make loans under programs administered and reviewed by the Veterans Administration, Department of Housing, Department of Urban Development, etc.

How do any of these regulatory bodies really know what's happening in America's banks?

In some instances, written reports signed by bank officers are periodically required. Examiners who visit banks play major roles. All regulatory agencies have agreed on an examination plan. Examination results obtained by one agency are provided to all others interested. The nice thing about this system is that it establishes a single examining authority, yet it does not prevent other regulatory authorities from conducting their own reviews. For example, if Comptroller of the Currency examiners discovered problems with a national bank, both the Federal Reserve and the FDIC could conduct their own independent exams if they felt such action was necessary.

Don't leave this chapter thinking that the only reason an agency examines a bank is to uncover dishonesty by bank personnel. Examiners perform an evaluation of the bank's reporting systems for all assets, liabilities, income and expenses. They check to see that the bank is complying with all related laws and regulations. How effective is its management? That's an important question they try to answer by observing policies and procedures which are in effect. The adequacy of the bank's capital is assessed. By studying each bank's capital and surplus, both stockholders and depositors are better ensured that the institution can withstand losses (i.e., bad loans).

The following four questions basically summarize what a bank exam answers:

1. What is the bank's true financial condition?
2. Are all related laws and regulations observed?
3. Is money available to sufficiently support bank operations?
4. What improvements can be made?

Question #4 deserves a little more explanation. Bank examiners try to identify ways in which the bank could operate more profitably. They look for ways to correct any weaknesses. Also, they may recommend measures which will help the bank better serve its customers' needs.

A copy of every report prepared by government examiners is always submitted to the bank's board of directors. Usually, the latter will then forward these reports to the bank's day-to-day management team.

What discussion about the banking community would be complete without introducing such terms as "branches" and "electronic terminals?"

Not all of these popular buzz words are limited to commercial banks. Many, as you'll soon discover, may also be applied to S&Ls.

Did you ever hear the term "unit banking state"? Some states allow a bank to do business only at one office location.

On the other hand, many subscribe to the branching philosophy. A *branch* is just a physical extension of the main bank. It's another office. Shopping malls are popular sites for branches. States which allow branching may still prohibit a free-for-all environment. By this, we mean that perhaps a bank will only be allowed to open branches within so many miles of the main office.

Both banks and S&Ls can be impacted by unit banking and branching laws. But do the same rules always apply? No. Some states allow S&Ls to have statewide branching, but prohibit commercial banks from doing the same.

Bank holding companies are another alternative in some states. A bank holding company is a separate, non-bank corporation that owns one or more banks. A state may allow one-bank holding companies or multi-bank holding companies. As its name implies, the latter can own more than one bank.

High-tech wizards have made banking more convenient than our grandparents ever dreamed it could be! Electronic terminals popularly referred to as ATMs (Automatic Teller Machines) are legal in many states. Located everywhere from airport terminals to grocery stores, customers may use specially issued plastic cards and passwords to make deposits and withdrawals. Depending on state law, both banks and S&Ls may establish these terminals. Some ATMs may even be used to pay bills at department stores, with the bank or S&L acting as agent for handling of the payment function.

What's the hottest topic in the financial community?

It's probably interstate banking. Interstate banking means that a bank in one state sets up offices in another. Rather than opening branches, one approach may be buying banks across state lines. Some states have already passed laws allowing interstate activity if a reciprocal agreement exists. By this, we mean that interstate activity can occur only with those states agreeable to allowing acquisitions in their areas by the same states. For example, Ohio may have a reciprocal agreement with Pennsylvania. If California is not included in this agreement, then a California bank may not set up business in either Ohio or Pennsylvania. On the other hand, the latter two states are allowed to buy banks or perhaps open offices in each other's states.

Interstate banking, whatever form it eventually takes, is certain to change the industry forever. Many in the financial community speculate that it will vastly decrease the number of commercial banks. We do not know what the end result will be. All we can safely say is that banking is an industry going through many transformations. Deregulation, interstate banking, increased computerization, and competition from non-banking entities definitely make it an industry worth watching.

Chapter 16

Insurance: How Important Is It?

H ow important is it for your bank deposits to be federally insured?

Any bank can fail. Very few banks do collapse, but there are no guarantees your bank will always remain stable.

Although the above observation may sound extremely harsh, we're trying to make a point — it's important that you select a bank backed by the Federal Deposit Insurance Corporation (FDIC).

During the Great Depression, hundreds of banks closed their doors. Many never reopened. Depositors lost millions of dollars. Family fortunes were wiped out almost overnight. People panicked. They descended in hordes upon what banks remained opened to demand withdrawal of their deposits. The banking industry was caught in a whirlwind of calamity.

On March 4, 1933, President Franklin D. Roosevelt issued a Presidential proclamation to temporarily close all banks. Restoring public confidence in America's banking system suddenly became a top priority of our country's highest office. People had to be convinced to stop withdrawing their money; otherwise, a nationwide bank collapse was inevitable.

In 1933, during Roosevelt's temporary closing of all banks, Congress enacted legislation authorizing creation of the FDIC. The FDIC is an independent agency of the U.S. Government.[1] Established to insure bank deposits, initially each account was insured for $5,000. Over the years, coverage has been increased to $100,000.

Are all banks insured by the FDIC?

No. Deposits in *all* national banks are covered by the FDIC. Deposits in *most* State banks, including commercial and mutual savings banks, are also insured along with deposits in some U.S. branches of foreign banks.

How do you know whether your bank is FDIC insured?

Insured banks are required to display the official FDIC sign at each teller location.

As a depositor in an FDIC-insured bank, *you* do not pay for deposit insurance. Your bank pays for the cost of this insurance through semiannual assessments based on its volume of deposits. The FDIC's insurance fund for covering deposits in banks which do fail consists of these assessments and income from the investment of the fund's balances. If a bank does fail, realize that prior to using FDIC funds all of the bank's assets are liquidated. Only if the liquidated assets will not pay each account the maximum coverage allowed are FDIC funds used. Payments to depositors usually begin within a few days after the date of a bank's final closing.

Let's define what type of accounts are subject to FDIC insurance.

All types of deposits normally received by a bank are insured. These deposits include all types of savings, checking, club, CDs, uninvested trust funds, certified checks, money orders and drafts, cashiers' checks, officers' checks, and letters of credit. Even travelers' checks for which an insured bank is primarily liable are covered.

As we said earlier, each account is insured for $100,000. Does this mean that if you have a regular savings and an MMIC both are insured for $100,000 therefore affording you $200,000 protection? It depends on account ownership.

If you have more than one account in the same bank in your name, these accounts are insured for a total of $100,000. Note that we did not say "each" is insured for the maximum. However, there is almost no limit to the amount that can be covered by FDIC protection if you but practice a few simple tricks.

To illustrate our point, we'll use the Lee family. Through account ownership variations, Bill and Jean Lee can easily obtain $300,000 FDIC insurance at just one institution.

By establishing accounts under three different ownerships, the Lee family secured substantially more insurance protec-

---

[1]The Federal Savings and Loan Insurance Corporation (FSLIC) is another governmental agency. This agency insures most savings and loan institutions to $100,000 per account.

tion. For example, if only the joint account existed and $300,000 was deposited, then $200,000 would be uninsured. In other words, if the bank failed there is no guarantee the Lee family will recover $200,000 of the $300,000 on deposit in that one joint account. However, by spreading the $300,000 among accounts held under different ownerships then the entire amount is guaranteed.

Another way to increase insurance coverage is to establish accounts at different FDIC backed banks. If you have accounts in several different insured banks, the balances *will not* be added together for the purpose of determining coverage. However in the case of a bank having one or more branches, the main office and all branches are considered to be one institution.

Let's recap what we've said. FDIC coverage guarantees you will recover deposits up to $100,000 if you bank fails. Such coverage may be increased two ways:

1. Establish accounts using different ownerships.
2. Establish accounts at different banks subscribing to FDIC coverage.

One note of interest we would like to add. Many people are concerned about establishing accounts in one name. In case of illness or other unusual circumstances, it can be difficult for anyone else to access funds. A Power of Attorney may be advisable if individual accounts are maintained. This document can authorize you to act as an agent for someone else. Your lawyer can assist in the preparation of a Power of Attorney.

Account Ownership	Maximum Coverage
Bill Lee (individual)	$100,000
Jean Lee (individual account)	$100,000
Bill Lee and Jean Lee (joint account)	$100,000
	$300,000

Can a bank terminate its membership with the FDIC?

Yes, but prior notice is always given to depositors. Also, insurance protection does not stop immediately after termination; it continues up to two years on deposits existing at the date of termination, less subsequent withdrawals, up to the $100.000 maximum.

How is FDIC coverage affected if one bank assumes another bank's deposits?

Mergers and purchases as well as takeovers following failures can suddenly change which bank you're doing business with. If your deposits are assumed by another insured bank, checking and regular savings deposits held in the original institution continue to be separately insured for a period of six months. Assumed time deposits (i.e., CDs) are insured to the earliest maturity date after the six-month period. Let's say you have $80,000 in an MMIC at Main Street Bank. The latter is purchased by First National Bank where you have $40,000 in an MMIC. You now have a total of $120,000 on deposit at First National Bank. Since the $80,000 existed prior to First National assuming Main Street's deposits, the entire sum of $120,000 is insured for a period of six months from the date of purchase.

FDIC insurance provides peace of mind to depositors. Banks approved for deposit insurance must meet high standards of safety and soundness in banking practices. Adherence to these standards is determined through regular bank examinations by Federal or State agencies.

In today's financial marketplace there are many competitors for your dollars. The combination broker/banker/insurance outlet is on the rise. The Kroger chain has already started all-purpose financial service centers inside their grocery stores in certain key cities. Sears department stores are actively marketing financial services; only in California, however, are banking services presently provided. Private corporations are actively petitioning Congress to liberalize relevant laws, to allow the establishment of more non-traditional financial centers. It seems as if everyone wants to get in the banking business these days!

As more players enter the banking game, learning to distinguish the different types of insurance in existence becomes a more critical issue in your financial planning. Private insurance funds and the FDIC are not the same. Deposits insured by private sources may be perfectly secure. However, only the FDIC (or FSLIC in the case of S&L's) is supported by a government agency. If you are unsure as to whether you bank is covered, ask the Federal Deposit Insurance Corporation (202-393-8400). For S&Ls, contact the Federal Home Loan Bank Board (202-377-6000).

Appendices

APPENDIX — POPULAR DEPOSITS INSTRUMENTS FOR CUSTOMERS

Marketed by banks nationwide, these deposit instruments represent available investment options for consumers.

Checking Accounts
- Regular
- NOW
- MMIC
- MM (better known as "SuperNOW")

Savings Accounts
- Regular (sometimes called "passbook")
- TDOA (also known as "open-time savings accounts")
- Christmas Club
- Vacation

CDs

IRAs

U.S. Securities
- U.S. Savings Bonds
- Treasury Bills
- Treasury Notes
- Treasury Bonds
- various agency bonds

APPENDIX — ENDORSEMENTS FOR
NEGOTIABLE INSTRUMENTS

Ownership of a negotiable instrument may be transferred by means of endorsements. This transfer of rights to another party is called "negotiation." A check is one of the most popular instruments we endorse.

There are four principal kinds of endorsements.

Blank Endorsement — Only the signature of the instrument's previous holder is required.

John L. Doe

Special Endorsement — The previous holder names the party to whom rights are being transferred and then signs the instrument.

Pay to the order of
Harry Jones
John L. Doe

In our above example, John L. Doe is giving ownership of this instrument to Harry Jones.

Restrictive Endorsement — The instrument's holder, in addition to signing it, identifies the purpose of the transfer and therefore restricts how the transferred instrument may be used.

For deposit only
John L. Doe

This sample endorsement specifies that the instrument can only be deposited. It cannot be negotiated for cash.

Restrictive endorsements are often combined with special endorsements. For example, John L. Doe, to whom a check is payable, may endorse it "Pay to First National Bank, for deposit only."

Pay to the order of
Harry Jones
for deposit only
John L. Doe

In the above example, the instrument is transferred to Harry Jones. However, he must deposit the proceeds rather than receive cash.

Qualified Endorsement — This type of endorsement limits the endorser's liability. Blank, special, and restrictive endorsements guarantee an instrument's value. By using such endorsements, you are agreeing to pay the instrument's amount if it is dishonored. To disavow this liability, a qualified endorsement must be used. The words "without recourse" or words of similar warranty must precede a qualified endorser's signature.

Pay to First National Bank
without recourse
John L. Doe

With the exception of a qualified endorsement, an endorser promises to pay the value of that instrument to the next holder (or any subsequent party) if, for any reason, the instrument is dishonored. Without such a guarantee, millions of dollars could not be safely exchanged each day for paper documents.

The Uniform Commercial Code (commonly referred to as the UCC) contains specific details indicating how to make transfers of negotiable instruments. It also governs policies related to endorsements. In addition to the basic ones we've illustrated, the UCC allows other forms besides handwritten endorsements. Both typewritten and rubber-stamped endorsements are valid under UCC guidelines and are accepted by most financial institutions.

Index